AWAKENING MY
Spiritual Heart

MANDI J NELSON

Copyright © 2019 Mandi J Nelson
First published in Australia in 2019
by MMH PRESS

www.mmhpress.com
www.karenmcdermott.com.au

All rights reserved. No part of this book may be used or reproduced by any means, graphic, electronic, or mechanical, including photocopying, recording, taping or by any information storage retrieval system without the written permission of the copyright owner except in the case of brief quotations embodied in critical articles and reviews.

Disclaimer: This book is a memoir. It reflects the author's present recollections of experiences over time. Some names and characteristics have been changed, some events have been compressed, and some dialogue has been recreated. Every length has been taken to protect the identity to protect those connected to this story. If you have any concerns please submit them in writing to the author and/or publisher.
The author and publisher have presented this book to the world with the intention of assisting others on their journey.

National Library of Australia Catalogue-in-Publication data:
Awakening My Spiritual Heart/Mandi J Nelson
Non Fiction - Inspirational

ISBN: (sc) 978-0-6486984-6-3
ISBN: (e) 978-0-6486984-7-0

CONTENTS

Acknowledgment   5
Foreword   7

Chapter One: Learning Self-love   13
Chapter Two: Finding my way home to truth   33
Chapter Three: Taking what wasn't mine   47
Chapter Four: Path to purity and right use of energy   53
Chapter Five: Learning to let go   70
Chapter Six: Path of purification   79
Chapter Seven: Satisfaction   87
Chapter Eight: The Path of An Explorer   97
Chapter Nine: Through the Looking Glass, what do I see?   103
Chapter Ten: I Surrender   113
Chapter Eleven: They Surrendered   120
Chapter Twelve: Through Movement I Connect and Ground   133
Chapter Thirteen: Breathe with me   141
Chapter Fourteen: Senseless   148
Chapter Fifteen: Single Point of Focus   154
Chapter Sixteen: Finding that Massive space Within   163
Chapter Seventeen: Lightening the mind   170

Afterword   185
Epilogue   191
Discovery List   193
About the author   195

ACKNOWLEDGMENT

I take this opportunity to Acknowledge and Honour the Traditional Spiritual Custodians of the land I was blessed to be born upon, Whadjuk Country in the Southwest of Western Australia.

I Acknowledge and Honour the Bibblemirn, or the Paperbark People, the Ancient Ones, the Ancestors, and the Elders both Past and Present.

In particular, I Acknowledge and Honour an Elder who has mentored and guided me and offered me incredible love and support, Violet Newman, whom I lovingly call 'Nanna Violet.'

I Acknowledge and Honour all the rich Knowledge and Wisdom I am Blessed to carry within this physical body, through my DNA, that flows through my body to the beat of my Ancestral drum, my heartbeat.

I Acknowledge and Honour all the rich Knowledge and Wisdom that you, as the Reader carry within your DNA, that you bring to this creation, as it flows through your body to the beat of your Ancestral Drum, your Heartbeat.

And in this I Acknowledge and Honour that co-joined through the Delivery and Receptivity of this information, a third and much more powerful Vector is Co-created, this point where we all meet… the zero point from which All evolves.

Finally, I Acknowledge and Honour the Animal, Plant, Feathered, Crystal, and Mineral Kingdoms, the Divas and the Nature Spirits, Father Sun, Beautiful Pachamama, Grandmother Moon, and Great Spirit, Source of All that is. And I humbly thank all of my Teachers and my Teachers' Teachers.

With Grace, I have infinite Gratitude to my Greatest teachers of all, my two children, Kael and Aala, who taught me why I needed to keep pulling myself out of the black hole, to keep striving to be the best version of myself I ever could or would be.

FOREWORD

We come in from a place far, far away, from hydrogen and helium atoms. 'Self-organising dynamics of the universe.' People say our known universe formed fourteen billion years ago. Galactic Intelligence through Dark Matter infuses us, coming from perhaps a six or seven stellar star system. Or maybe the space quantum physics refers to as Nothingness from which All is created. As a tiny molecule of star light from the Milky Way, we come spinning in through the infinite universe, from a galaxy way beyond the imaginings of the contained and educated human mind. A minute particle of stardust careening past the planets that make up Earth's star system, where the sun and the planets have formed together from a curtain of gas and dust. Journeying through the sky, through the clouds, and the wind, traverse across valleys, mountains, hills, the plateaus, and plains. We are the dance of the breeze upon the leaves of the trees, and the varying shades of chlorophyll green the kaleidoscope sunlight casts upon them. We descend grounded in the Earth, the ruby red clay of canyons and iron-rich soils, the densest and darkest mineral bountiful browns, silky volcanic blacks. We merge with the shiny, golden stalagmites and stalactites of caves and the brilliant white diamond sparkling sand. We come down into the water systems, from the rain as it falls from the skies frolicking. We are the waves upon the ocean, the currents in the rivers, the trickle in the streams, the power and momentum in the waterfalls, the dense stillness of the lakes. We are the star ignited in its fusion furnace, the majestic flames of the fire, sent to warm and ignite the planet. We come into the cites all over the world and the small country towns, into places of All the Nations, with our rainbow-coloured ways. We are found in the Red, the White, the Yellow and the Black; we are the messengers of Love sent here to Awaken the Spiritual

Heart.

Our tools are those that offer humanity the ability to step out of the Illusion of the mind and the programming of society. To have the perceptiveness to sense a little more than the eye can see, the nose can smell, the ears can hear, the fingers can touch, the tongues can taste. We are just beyond that which you have been trained and taught to perceive. We hold Cosmic Consciousness found through past wisdom and philosophy, the stories of the Ancient Ones, and those of the Elders. And we are beyond the false impression and propaganda that is perpetuated to maintain the status quo - not the Primary Universal Law of Growth, evolution or involution. They deliver us through Creation, music, art, dance, the animals, the medicine of plants, the elements, the nature spirits. We come via meditation and yoga, through stillness, and self-reflection, self-inquiry and love. We come into individual bodies through an interconnected web, blasting out from the stellar nebula, with independent roles, from the one Galactic Consciousness. We came from far, far away to awaken humanity to their own capacity for freedom, from stars that give birth to the Elements. We come through to the human bodies who can best serve the purpose, birthed from the stars through the elements of hydrogen, helium, phosphorus, carbon and nitrogen. Bodies that are the Temples and Shrines to Exploration of Consciousness.

We weave and dance through these threads of stories of Ancient Wisdom made modern. Within the simplicity may you find that which you resonate with, to inspire you to open your heart to your own Spiritual Awakening. The underlying fabric of this piece of work is based on Patanjali's sutras because so much of my personal growth has stemmed from a yoga Sadhana. It has literally been the Golden Thread that interwove the pieces together. And because traditionally, this is how our wisdom was always shared through the myths and legends, often verbally around campfires. Some stories are a messy overflow, like the bobbin-jammed-cotton thread that spills out beyond the edge of the cloth, all tangled chaotic and twisted. Others just barely touch the material in how Patanjali might have intended.

Patanjali's 'sutras' were written somewhere between a couple of centuries before or up to first or second BCE, and consists of about 1200 words, in 195 sutras. The term 'sutra' means thread whereby the maximum amount of information would be placed in the smallest amount of words. The 'essence' if you like. We are purely focussing on a couple of those sutras where he refers to the eight limbs of yoga. It is important to note, mainly if this concept of Eight Limbs of Yoga is new for you, there are infinite numbers of different translations of Patanjali's work. And a boundless amount of opinion over when it was first penned as mostly this information would have been shared from Guru to Disciple.

My first introduction to the 'eight limbs' was a feeling like I was meeting someone I knew before with that warm degree of familiarity and recognition. An 'aha' moment. I always knew there was 'more' to yoga. I actively sought those teachers who would sate my appetite for this. Their teachings gave me a 'whiff,' and I became hungry to get to the source. I have the most profound and solemn regard for Sage Patanjali and his work; it is what I form the basis of my practice on. What follows is not intended to be a rewrite of his philosophy. It merely provides a forum through which to channel these stories of growth and change together. Yoga has always been the 'reset' point through which my 'life' interwove through. Patanjali's sutras became the vehicle for my narrative for a greater simplicity of reading because the mind likes to build a form around things that have no relationship. Through my explorative path of spirituality throughout my Earth-walk, this is for me the one that fits the closest. It is clear, but not dictatorial. Yoga has so much to offer us than exercise - it is a way of expanding your consciousness and Awakening your Spiritual Heart.

These are my stories I've put together in a way to create more meaning for the reader, perhaps offering new ways for you to 'unpack' your own life.

May you find the inspiration to live and write your own, or to live your life more simply from the Heart, in the space of Collective Consciousness.

I humbly, thank you, the Reader, for gifting your time and energy to share this space.

In loving kindness
Mandi J Nelson

*All music referred to in the beginning of the chapters can be listened to by joining my Spotify playlist Awakening My Spiritual Heart[1] by Mandi J Nelson.

*There are **bonus** sequences links, yoga pose, meditation and breath practices that some links are **only** for book purchases **and** a Special 'Healing' meditation to download[2].

---

1. https://open.spotify.com/user/12143591576/playlist/4DN6N1hNH5BPSctP50Y-j9M?si=GCHK5KDpRkWBzDsCFv53rA
2. Link to bonus - special healing/activation https://youtu.be/dQUzyKw5LJs

Patanjali'S 8 LIMBS OF YOGA

Chapter One

LEARNING SELF LOVE

Ahimsa

Playlist - REM - Losing My Religion 1991

In 1993, in the streets of Applecross, Perth, Western Australia, near the Derbil Yerrigan, (Swan River) a canary-yellow roller-skate-looking car screeches to a halt in the middle of the road. In synchronisation, a cloud passes over the sun, and the sky darkens above the rich and royal mauve bloom of the Jacaranda flowers. Out jump two scantily clad, skinny, screeching, hissing, hollowed cheekbones, sunken-eyed individuals from either side of the car. They are male and female, and one is me. With pin-pricked pupils, purple mash on my inner arms, I have an 'eight-ball' of speed in my top my boyfriend is trying to forcibly retrieve from me. A game of cat and mouse around and over the car ensues. Though this mouse is as prepared to kill as the cat. It is a vicious, nasty confrontation where the 'standard' rules of human interaction had departed for good. We are snarling, baring teeth, kicking, and scratching one another. I will not give up the drugs, and he will not give up trying to get them. Amid this serene street, we stand hurling expletives at one another, missiles exploding in what used to be each of our hearts. The source of love for one another, our weapons are swear words so bad I care not to repeat them today. We verbally expunge the toxicity of the drug we have injected for the past two sleepless weeks. We are hatred personified.

There is no love left between us or in amongst us. We are shells of What We Once Were; Shadows only. We are beyond the Light and now traverse in the pit of debasement. Like two vultures circling one another, we waited for the other one to let up so they can have access to the prize. We no longer had time for the companionate expressions of a couple. Our brief beginning days of tenderness, of sharing and caring had dissipated in direct proportion to the escalation of our binge, and our descent into the depths of depravity. We have moved beyond natural laws of loving kindness and exist in the realms of many caught in the addiction cycle - ultimate serving of self, first and foremost. At Any Cost.

Warwick and I met in the detox centre, east of the city. He was a much bigger junkie than me, notorious, and played with the 'big boys' of the Perth drug scene. His appetite for drugs after using for numerous years was insatiable. His high threshold enabled him to shoot up speed anywhere between five to ten times a day, on a 'good' day. Then he used smack (heroin) to come down as it eased the harshness.

Like many with an advanced degree in drug use, 'dealing' drugs to others became the chosen way to feed his addiction. As he was using lots of drugs, he needed to deal lots of drugs to keep his habit fed which exponentially raised his odds of getting caught. Hardly surprising, Warwick had a criminal record as long as his arm, was 'well known' by police, youth workers and the general 'scene' in Perth.

In comparison, I was naïve, unknown and reasonably 'fresh' regarding 'junkiedom,' perhaps best described as 'an almost 3rd-year psychology major uni student who had taken the summer a bit hard'. The 'Extreme Experimentalist.' I made a choice at a pertinent, 'two forks in the road' time in space over the latter portion of summer in a moment of clarity, of my own free will. I recognised my use was escalating and had a distinct realisation I could, at that *very* moment, still pull back from my 'use'. Life could go back to the way it once was. Or, I could continue my descent into the world of drugs.

At that very juncture, *I made the conscious choice, voluntarily, to investigate the latter.*

Interestingly, almost everyone I've spoken to who's walked a similar path and lived to tell the tale, agree they too made a conscious choice to become a junkie. It wasn't like a big hole they fell into by accident and then woke up one day and realised they were in a ditch. It was a big hole they chose to fall into, a warlike trench they walked into, just as I made a choice to step down into it too. The decision to plummet and flay dismally like a caught fish in a bucket, however, *only* became a 'viable' option after the repeated self-medication of drugs. Originally used as escapism and fun, they initially made me feel so good. Then eventually they punctured my self-worth and pierced my etheric field, allowing both to be open to entity attachment. And subsequent poor life choices. Until I needed them to just see the light of the day.

Which was all very well and good for me - to choose a deliberate descent. My loved ones could do nothing but stand around, mouths agape, at how quickly my life spiralled downwards over the three-month uni break from December to February. Their once radiant, joyous, extroverted and open daughter removed, this sullen, secretive, sneaky and jumpy version in her place. Or witness the 'high,' over the top, talking at one hundred miles an hour, jittery and paranoid version. To watch as the months ensued, and the degeneration gained rapid, serious momentum in a train-wreck kind of capacity.

We knew this was the crescendo of a rather long descent spanning for the best part of a decade. It might have sprung from an innate pioneering and inquisitive nature expressed since day dot. From the moment I first walked, I needed strong boundaries because of my intrinsic curiosity and compulsion to explore the unknown. Others pulling me back with the rein from self-harm meant enforced boundaries rather than self-discovered ones. My close network of family and friends had no preparation for the rough and jagged terrain I'd taken us on.

When I first met Warwick in the detox centre, I'd been using amphetamines for just over five months. After deciding to 'follow the path' I 'hooked up' with a minor dealer, Steve. I met him in a club as a 'bunny' wherein the bottom line, the relationship comprised of me trading sex for drugs. Though we used terms of love, 'babe,' 'honey,' 'sugar-pie,' there wasn't a lot of kindness nor deep affection between us.

Sure, we shared experiences, picking up amphetamines and ecstasy from the dealers, then passing it on to those who wanted to 'score'. We went to raves - me to dance, him to deal, though it wasn't what you would call a 'healthy relationship' built upon foundations of mutual concern, care, and loving gestures. I guess you could say we shared the same common interest. To inject amphetamines without 'paying' for it. I had the car; he had the contacts.

I didn't 'care' for this guy. You couldn't say there was a fondness… though neither at this point was I 'caring' or that fond of nor kind to myself. If I was truthful, Steve reminded me of a slug. I saw him as a means to an end. I'd cultivated myself quite the habit that exceeded my capacity to pay for. So, it required I either turn to prostitution, crime, or find a dealer to assist me. Synchronicity stepped in when Steve and I met at a club just as I was running out of the speed I'd ripped off some dealers in a country town. So, he appeared for me at the 'right' time for me to continue deepening my demonic dance with the drug.

I don't know what Steve was like when he wasn't using because I never knew him from that perspective. I only knew he was quick to temper, with a faster penchant for violence, a slap across the face, a push down the stairs. He thought it was fun to slip a 'rowie' (date rape drug) into my drink. Then he could use me in whatever manner he desired without the capacity of protesting or refusing. It was challenging to command respect when the truth of it was if it weren't for the drugs, I wouldn't be there. And we both knew it.

I recall my parents finding out where we were 'holed' up in a house in the eastern suburbs of Perth, having heard he'd beaten me at some point. The guy whose house it was answered, and I spoke to my mum and dad at the doorway for a few moments. It was enough for them to see my broken doll-like, pathetic state to persuade me to come with them. Then Steve came to the door, told them to "Fuck off," that I was old enough to make my own decisions as I cowered behind him. My mum and dad tried many negotiating tactics, coaxing and wheedling with Steve to no avail. He refused to let us talk to one another any further. And refused any of their suggestions. This infuriated my mother so much she 'lost the plot.' She screeched and lurched her five foot nothing, thin frame at him, trying to scratch him or hit him in the face. My dad held her back, though he too was so furious he almost took to hitting Steve with a baseball bat. Steve threatened to call the police, and they unwillingly left, letting me know I could come home at any time. I only had to call. It is beyond my imagination as a now-parent how harrowing and distressful that drive home would have been.

I ended up staying with the guy to take more than a few extra beatings, and to inject myself many more times over. Weeks later, after landing in a crumpled heap at the bottom of the stairs again, I found myself crying and shaking out of fear, coming 'down' off the latest binge. I swallowed ten Panadol tablets in a misguided suicide attempt. Then I squared myself for the briefest of glimpses in the smeared, dirty mirror and realised I no longer wanted this lifestyle. It wasn't working for me. That maybe I should give a shit about driving around with enough speed in my car to ensure I got locked up for a long time. Jail wasn't a 'good' option out of this lifestyle. I needed to get myself out. And I deserved to offer myself more. So much more. I understood I needed to scrounge up whatever iota of self-love remained and pull myself out of this situation as quickly as I could. It was time to pick myself back up. I'd tried the 'bunny' option to keep the drugs flowing, to keep my addiction fed. I was no longer prepared to sacrifice any more of 'me' to experiment with hard crime or real prostitution. I enlisted the help of my grateful, concerned and at that stage, very fearful parents. They came and assisted a much slighter, tear-stained, unkempt and fragmented version of their daughter. With her came her scant belongings overflowing in ripped plastic bags to move out while Steve was out of the house.

Upon getting me home, they had absolutely no idea of what to do with this 'coming down' psychotic version as I alternated between tears, paranoia and verbal abuse. If you visualise Amy-Winehouse- meets-the-Exorcist-meets-a cat-on-the -prowl, that ought to give you the gist. I was a messy conflict of desires. At one moment, sure about my decision to stop my drug use, the next crawling the walls, trying to find my confiscated keys to go 'score' more 'go-ey.' They made a few phone calls and convinced me to see our family doctor before doing anything else. By a pure stroke of luck, she found there was a space for me in the In-Patient Withdrawal Unit I'd heard about in the city after the weekend.

I was incredibly blessed to make plans to get there on Monday to begin my supervised withdrawal. In the meantime, it was just a case of getting me through the next couple of days and nights. She wrote a script for Valium for me to assist with the process, to take the edge off and calm down perhaps enough to entertain sleep.

It sounds straightforward in retrospect, but it wasn't. That weekend was pure hell for all of us. My younger siblings, two sisters and a brother, witnessed all my behaviours. The nuts and bolts of it were, I was addicted to speed and to putting a needle into my veins. To the whole process of injecting. I was so caught up in self-abasement. So incredibly self-absorbed, no one else existed at that point except me. My parents allowed me to go score that weekend and trusted I would come home, that I wouldn't go back to Steve, nor make any further attempts at my life too.

I was used to using three to four times a day with a habit of about two hundred dollars when I was with Steve and being beaten. Suddenly I was back at home with the folks and apparently no longer using. Amphetamines were no longer on tap and my 'use' which I had initially embarked upon in the name of fun and freedom, had now enslaved me. It wasn't pretty.

I was a moving, lifelike stick-figure, weighing in at thirty-eight kgs, looking like I'd just acted in the movie Schindler's List. A walking billboard for either severe illness, drug abuse or anorexia. Perhaps a little of all three as I would sometimes go for days without eating when I was 'high' - I didn't need to. At a brief glance, it was apparent to all there was 'stuff' going on for me. I was the customer shop assistants maintained a close eye on, and security regularly checked my bag and pockets before I left the shop. To my parents and brother and sisters, I must have been like a 'walk-in' to the person they knew before.

By the Grace of God, we all made it through that crazy weekend. Me in a not dissimilar state I'd been in for the last five months, heavily under the influence of drugs. They were fearful not only for my life but as I was in the house, probably theirs too. I made it to my Monday induction to the Central Drug Unit, where I would stay to detox under medical supervision over the next seven days. I turned up 'on,' high as a kite as I swan-song like, injected myself with the last of the speed I had in the family bathroom at 6am before we left. It was my final goodbye, or so I thought.

Despite these messy, soul-destroying and heartbreaking experiences I created and endured, I was a 'recreational junkie', just borderline, flirting with drug use. The professionals considered my usage to be severe enough to be under supervised medical care to detox off speed. Before I met Warwick, I hadn't yet fallen into the black bowels beyond the earth, the very depths of despair and desperation. I was twenty-two years old with about five months of escalating drug use on my Curriculum Vitae. Warwick was a little younger, though as an adoptee, he'd been remonstrating with his demons through drug use for so much longer. It was an instant attraction.

Despite his defecation to self, he was an attractive young man with long, curly jarrah-brown hair, average height, muscular build, olive skin, and oval-shaped deep green eyes. Exuding Presence and Charisma, whatever space he moved into, he 'owned' it by simply entering it. He continued to maintain the eye's interest by his incessant movement created by his hyperactivity and previous excessive speed use, yet also had a quiet natural way about him. He was the type to be still shaking a leg while sitting still, and then could also be intense and broody.

Warwick and I connected on a spiritual level. We both had practiced yoga and meditation, and shared an interest in crystals, the esoteric, the magical and the mystical. We swapped many stories through the incessant cigarette smoke as we lit each afresh from the butt of another, leading to us spending a lot of time together that week. We drank copious amounts of heavily sugared instant coffee - creating an inferior relation of an amphetamine high - allowing us the opportunity of getting to know one another better. In the course of our conversation, he told me he was heading to a rehabilitation centre out of the city. On a 'bio-organic farm', it was primarily to get a more lenient sentence on a drug possession and dealing charge that had been reprimanded though he would inevitably face.

I had not thought about going to 'rehab' until I met Warwick. My thoughts centred on my predicament with drugs, and the desperate volatile and destructive relationship I was in. I could barely think past not needing to find my next hit. I also knew I no longer had the means to service my habit. Somewhere through the space of my involvement with Steve, in amongst the escalating speed use, I dared to attend a domestic violence counselling session after taking another vicious beating. That's where I learned about the seven-day in-house withdrawal centre.

I could check in there if a bed was available as a form of escaping the demolition site my life was becoming. The counsellor explained this would provide me with the opportunities to get away from the toxic and brutal relationship I was in. It would help to gain some clarity for my next 'move' and provide a 'safe' space away from family, friends, 'triggers' and all that I knew to find something new. It was withdrawing in a 'safe' medically monitored clinic, creating the right set of circumstances that allowed space between me and my drug of choice. Through doing this, I could rebuild more solid foundations for my life.

Survival was the extent of my decision-making process when I met Warwick in the detox centre. Remove me from the drug and the relationship. Get clean. Make it through the weekend at my parents. Get into the CDU.

Way back over the summer break, I had chosen the path of a 'junkie,' to explore it, to see what would happen. This time my choices were reflecting the desire to live.

I had a vague idea about buying myself time to figure out what to do without the drugs, to discover who 'I' was again. In the emotional, physical, and mental space I'd created through my lifestyle in under six months, it was challenging to make clear decisions that wasn't around using. I'd gone from wanting to get my Masters and Ph.D. in Psychology to driving around with enough amphetamines to leave me in jail for a long time. Back then, that life in the gutter seemed like a good idea. I wasn't sure where I went from here. At Warwick's and some detox staff's suggestion, a rehabilitation centre for afterward began to look like a good option for me in more ways than one.

Through the help of the clinic I was withdrawing in, I explored different options available to foster more space between myself and the drug. After attending a few Narcotics Anonymous meetings and researching similar based live-in rehabilitation centres, I learned about their 'Twelve-step program'. While it seemed to help many, I had inherent issues with the first step and the underlying principle.

Regardless of the circumstances I had created for myself, I wouldn't and found I couldn't admit I was powerless over speed. Furthermore, I had issues handing my power over to 'God.' So, I needed something that sat outside of these parameters. When I discovered the 'farm', it seemed to tick more boxes than anything else offered. They primarily assisted one to empower oneself, provided some counselling and granting the opportunity to be out in the fresh air, on the land in all areas of a working farm that grew bio-organic fruits and vegetables.

The Farm encouraged you to take self-responsibility and guidance from your Higher Self. To find the strength from within, through hard work and discipline, through reflection and assistance from your 'co-workers' and staff. And it had the added bonus that Warwick would be there too. So, while still in the detox centre I began to make enquires how to go about getting offered a place there. I realised I needed a next 'step' to my plan as going back to my parents wasn't an option that would work for any of us short or long term.

I discovered attending the farm required participating in a series of interviews and counselling sessions set in their city office. One submitted 'wee tests' on the premises, in their toilet (so you couldn't use anyone else's pee). They demanded you 'prove' your 'mettle' and resolve by remaining drug free over a couple of weeks waiting time to get in. If you used, then you had to start the whole process over.

I spent the seven days at the detox centre, trying to re-establish some healthier options for my body as I physically worked through the withdrawals. My muscles twitched and ached, my temperature fluctuated, and my mood swings alternated between extreme anxiety, paranoia and depression. Participating in 'drug raves' (talking incessantly with other inpatients about drug experiences) though banned, was still indulged. It inevitably led to us all 'hanging out' and glorifying our involvement in the scene. Famished without the 'whizz', I began eating regularly and reasonably healthily. I attempted to regain a more regular sleeping pattern; trying to reinstate sleeping at night as a habit, and thankfully, they offered Valium to help with this. Speed doesn't lend itself to much sleep unless you're coming down.

I attended daily group meetings and had one-on-one sessions with a counsellor where I often cried as the reality of what had become my life began to sink in. It was such a mess. I didn't know where to piece it all back together again. The stories I shared with the counsellor sounded like some B-grade movie, and much of it filled me with shame and disgust.

Upon my successful week's completion at the detox centre, my parents collected me and took me to their coastal suburban house where my three younger siblings still lived. I was only one week clean, and very 'trigger happy,' very easy to 'fire up'. Although I wanted to go to the farm and was making preparations to attend, the past five months had taught me a different way of dealing with stress or altercation. To inject a substance into my body. To pop a tab. I had many moments of angered, heated words, emotionally blackmailing everyone around me.

I threatened if I didn't get my way, I would go score, thus thwarting my chances to go to the farm. Basically, being an 'arsehole' to my family around me. Lots of slamming doors and firecracker volatility.

Seven days is not a lot of time between you and the drug of your choice, even though when you are back at day one, day seven seems like a lifetime away. Your emotions are raw, sleep patterns out, invariably, diet is only just making its way to normality. It was a perilous time, where old familial wounds and patterns of behaviour began to resurface unbridled. I'd taken away my coping mechanism without yet figuring out new ways of managing. Thankfully, because of the Grace of God, the never-ending patience and probable prayer by my atheist parents, I made it through those two weeks. My next step of rehabilitation: using no drugs, nor creating any severe damage to myself or those around me.

I took my recovery a little more seriously when I committed to stay at the 'farm,' about an hour's drive out of Perth, for three months. I also agreed to not use any drugs, including alcohol, to be non-violent, nor to enter any sexual relationship with anyone while I was there. We would be in danger of 'transferring' our addiction from the drug to the other person if we did. The Farm encouraged a healthy lifestyle. We embraced each day at 6am to begin our duties. They invited us to work on the land to connect with the earth, to assist in the bio-organic fruit and vegetables' growth. It was a profitable working farm with weekly deliveries to the metro area.

All 'live-in's' had important and accountable jobs to do, positions, and responsibilities to uphold within our community. There was one-on-one counselling, group sessions, meetings, meditation sessions, doctors' appointments to attend and plenty of time for self-reflection, journaling, and forming friendships with others.

I concreted my daily practice of yoga asana and meditation in the first week or so of being at the farm. One of my other attractions to attending this rehab centre was that they weren't shoving religion down your throat. They encouraged you to find the strength from within and guidance from your 'higher self.' It was a time of immense growth for me.

When I arrived, I could barely look at myself in the mirror. I was that disgusted with what I saw reflected at me. That horrified, guilty, disappointed and shameful of what was on the inside, I point blank refused to have a mirror in my space for quite some time. I found it very difficult, almost impossible to face my image. Festering maggots of hate filled my body. And in the times I'd peeked a glimpse, I was awash with self-loathing.

My outer reflected my inner world. Pockmarked and hallowed, my skin and my haunted, raccoon-shadowed eyes showed what I had inflicted upon others and witnessed being cast, what I had seen and what I had done.

My body, which had always been healthy and capable, was skinny and ineffectual. Along with scarred, bruised veins, and random deep eggplant bruises on my legs I had little pus-filled sores. Those were from where I'd picked at the non-existent 'invisible insects' crawling over my body while high on speed. I had been down into the depths of depravity, into the bowels of humanity, where all that is good and right in the world is desecrated. Teeming with self-hatred, I found very little reflected in my eyes worthy of holding on to or seeing. I was all but dead.

Yet, from somewhere way deep inside, a tiny, watery, though crystal clear voice beckoned me to get back onto my life raft, to make my way to my yoga mat. To get into a practice of my asana and meditation.

I discovered yoga through books my dad's friend, Neils, left at our house when I was eight. He also left his convertible when he joined Bhagwhan Shree Rajneesh (the Sanyassians or Orange people) in the United States. My sister and I used to entertain one another in copying the more advanced poses in the books. This led to an interest in gymnastics for us both, an investment covering an eight-year practice for each, leading to elite-level performance and training. We trained twenty plus hours each a week, with coaching juniors for me. Both of our gymnastic endeavours and dreams of the Olympic Games came to an abrupt halt because of injury. On my part, at age fifteen, a broken arm around the elbow they couldn't reset properly despite trying twice; my sister a reoccurring pulled hamstring muscle.

This training meant I had been used to exercising. I'd listened to my body's needs and called upon the discipline yoga calls 'tapas' or internal fire required to commit to a daily practice and honouring of one's self. I knew what I needed to do to look after and train a physical body. And I knew I hadn't been in my exploration of the drug scene.

This inherent voice, burning brightly within, softly yet firmly suggested I get up at 5am every morning. I found some space for my 'self' in amongst this new busyness of the scheduling and communal lifestyle at the farm. It told me it was imperative to commit to finding time each day to dedicate to myself in the name of love, kindness and compassion. To rebuild my sense of purpose in the world and redefine who I was. And because I was in a space quiet enough for me to listen to that beautiful wee voice, for the first time in six months, I did.

One inhalation, one exhalation, one breath at a time. One asana, one Surya Namaskar[3] - sun salutation, one morning at a time. I built my Sadhana[4] as I built my strength. Starting basically with a couple of sun salutations and meditation, then gradually introducing more and more advanced asana. I began to notice my breath and how shallow it was - in fact, I barely inhaled - I was still smoking. I observed my thoughts, noting how negative they were through my asana and meditation practice. The mornings turned into weeks, the weeks into months. The love for my 'self' I held grew from that desolate, harsh desert where it is difficult for most lifeforms to thrive, to a minuscule tiny flicker, to a much larger flame. Just as the seasons we see in nature change. From summer to autumn, to winter to spring, from life to death and regeneration and rebirth, new green sprouts found form. I began to care more for my 'self', to unravel the pain, to look myself back in the eye. Surreptitiously, then with incrementally longer moments in the shared bathroom facility, I began the arduous process to forgive myself. To let go of the Past, to embrace the

---

3. link to Surya Namaskar - https://youtu.be/Qy5-tjOG7z8
4. Sadhana means practice

Present and to start to Dream of a future. I stopped dying, and my actions of self-love enabled growth again. Just as the barren trees sprout tiny bits of greenery in the spring as the sun warms again after a cold winter. Fresh shoots started to emerge as inspiration - messages from Spirit.

It took about a month's dedicated daily practice of asana and meditation to have the courage to introduce a mirror into my space at the farm. I gained the strength through my Sadhana to look at myself once more, to have the spunk to see what was before me. To soften a little, to let go of the tension in my jaw from constant grinding while using. To allow my shoulders to descend and unwind the mercurial last five months. And drop the past some more and remain with what was directly in front of me. My thoughts became less self-critical, less loathing, less shaming, and resentful. I consciously replaced the negativity with affirmations.

"I, Mandi, love, respect, and accept my body, mind and spirit."
"I am Here, and the Time is Now."
"I am asking my Higher Self for guidance."
"I choose to let go of negative thought patterns."
"I am safe. I am love. I am Loved"
"My body is the Temple of my Living Spirit."

And I began to love myself just a little more with each passing day. With building strength, I could hold Virabhadrasana 2 (Warrior 2)[5] for more significant amounts of breathing time. My atrophied legs became better able to bear weight against the earth or enfeebled arms could remain at shoulder height for longer lengths of time. Directly in synch, the more courage and strength that simultaneously grew off the mat in my day-to-day activity and interaction with others and life itself. I could lift more in the physical work required around the farm, and I embodied more of the attributes of that mighty warrior. As I practiced, I reminded myself of my might and my resolution, and so it grew. Many of the yogic asanas have mythical stories around them, and the one behind Warrior 2 is worth

---

5. link to Virabhadrasana 2 pose https://youtu.be/rlCiSlXjPiY

mentioning at this point. In terms of Sanskrit, Vira means 'Hero,' and Bhadra means 'Auspicious,' asana is the pose.

Set in ancient times in the celestial realms, the asana tale happened long, long ago. It is the story of a daughter (Sati) marrying a dreadlocked yogi (Lord Shiva). Her father (Daksha) disapproves, which leads to the consequences of her choices and her father's subsequent lack of acknowledgment over their union. After their marriage, Daksha holds a party inviting all from the heavenly realm, excluding his daughter and her husband. Sati suggests to her husband Shiva they should attend, though Shiva doesn't see the point, nor does he wish to anger her father anymore. Sati goes alone, and while there publicly suffers taunts from her father, who is holding court.

After being the brunt of his jokes and humiliated by the crowds' laughter, Sati declares as he has gifted her the physical body, she no longer wishes to claim it. Hence she falls into a mystic trance, increasing her inner fire through pranayama - yogic breath until her body bursts into flames. She combusts in front of her father and all of those at the party. Her husband learns of this and from a place of deep despair and anger, rips one of his dreadlocks out of his hair and creates a fierce warrior Vira Bhadra. He commands it to go to the party and destroy everyone there. Swiftly, the warrior creates mayhem and havoc, cutting off the head of Sati's father. Shiva arrives soon after and, remorseful at the disaster he witnesses at Vira's hand, rectifies the situation. He brings his love's father back to life, giving him the head of a goat. The guests and Daksha then honour him and this story finishes with Shiva leaving the party with the lifeless form of Sati in his arms.

This tale speaks of slaying the ego (Daksha) for the sake of the heart (Sati), similar to what I had to do to follow the truth of my path. I had to annihilate the hedonistic behaviour of addiction to be open to listening to the truth of my awakening spiritual heart.

The story behind one of my favourite poses at the time of recovering also touches upon themes of compassion, and the capacity for life renewed through forgiveness and humility. This is the same journey I embarked upon morning after morning of my Sadhana. I eventually came to a place where I could ultimately confront myself once more with less shame and disgust and with more Loving Kindness. At the root of this tale, is the underlying theme that even when we make mistakes in life we have the opportunity to put our best foot forward.

As in Warrior 2, we must do our utmost to do the right thing eventually. I naturally found an affiliation with Warrior poses without knowing the story or the meaning behind it. Somehow my body innately understood by practicing these poses daily, they would help increase my strength. They also gave me the fortitude I needed to flourish in this new direction in my life. They assisted me in destroying the negative self-talk, just as Shiva's dreadlock did. And they fostered the courage and resilience required for me to follow through on my decision to be 'clean' and to cultivate more compassion and integrity.

Likewise, the more I developed my practice of 'mindfulness meditation'[6], the more I could practice *being* with what I was experiencing, through my breath, the sounds, sensations, smells, textures, sight and taste. The hatred and violence I held towards myself and others dissipated. I learned to see beyond the pain filament shrouding my eyes, to avoid diving into the depths of stories past, to just be in the Present moment. I learned to re-inhabit my body, coming home, back to 'me.' When someone said something that triggered me, I tried to observe it rather than allowing myself to drop into a samskara - a behavioural pattern of reaction. I worked with a counsellor on my guilt, humiliation and shame, releasing stories that bound me to a destructive lifestyle. They'd kept me feeding and festering in the past, the very reason I sought release and freedom through drugs. I began to explore some suspected child sexual abuse through a friend of my parents with my counsellor. With the mirror's introduction into my room came the ability for me to see beyond my reflection, opening the door for others to also truly see me.

***

---

6. Link to example of mindfulness practice https://youtu.be/M3S9JhqQj1E

A good friend, and one of my spiritual influences, Alison Jarred, speaks about the physical body's experience of debasement. When it is so desecrated, defiled and dishonoured, it is not a clean enough vehicle for the 'spirit' or essence of the self to govern. She muses entities have attached to the being, utilising the vessel for its own purposes. To her, the drop in vibration caused by defilement brings you into resonance with the lower levels of the astral light. And, as per law of attraction, you attract entities of the same vibration. It is easy for them to become attached because drug and alcohol abuse cause thinning (and sometimes rips) to the aura providing easy entry past your natural protection of the auric cortex. Also, these lower states of consciousness have no filtering, no standards, and you become like an open sewer for whatever wants to flow through. Thus, it is effortless to become influenced and fed upon by these lower entities.

I can't help but wonder if in my case, this was why extreme drug use and an erratic, hedonistic lifestyle was so appealing to me. Or because of a complete lack of self-love and care, an entity or entities attached itself/themselves to me. When we were young, my sister and I toyed with Ouija boards and seances. One could also postulate that perhaps a lower vibrational being attached to my aura at that point, all those years ago. It offers a conceivable, rational solution to the conundrum why a former straight-A student became hell-bent on self-destruction.

It is also possible I was just destined to explore and experiment further than most, due to landing in this world in an unusual manner - feet first. Or that I just set about to fulfil the requirements of one of my Greatest Lessons of what I came here to explore. My very own Tree of Life, the first branch, the path of Ahimsa - Loving Kindness, first written about in yogic philosophy, Patanjali's sutras, the Eight limbs of yoga, the 'Yamas.'

Musings aside, thankfully, amid the Dark Night of my Soul, I heard the whispering of Great Spirit, and Source of All that is through to the Essence of what I truly am. The codes ignited by the Divine, drawn down via Father Sun, set a Golden yellow spark alight in my mini-sun. This was my Manipura, the solar plexus centre for self-worth and for radiating power. With this rekindling, I began to move forward, gaining confidence

I would make positive decisions to improve my life. Initially, it is what gave me the courage to leave the catastrophic circumstances I'd created with Steve. Then the re-enlightenment of the Manipura instigated a revival of the lower and upper chakra, allowing self-love to be re-awakened in the Anaharta, heart chakra. I expressed and practiced through non-violence to self or others, contributing to the Awakening. This led me to find my way back to a daily yogic practice of asana, meditation and self-reflection. Spirit's way back to 'self' and to re-inhabit my body was to re-introduce standards of self-care, of discipline, kindness and self-love.

For me, that deep practice of ahimsa and compassion stemmed from the daily tapas of prayer to my temple (body) upon the mat after hovering on the very cliff edge of total dismantling. I remember first hearing the whole concept of the human body being a temple, and it sparked a great deal of resonance for me. The way I'd trashed my personal space of worship made me sad and embarrassed. Through various declining degrees of disrespect since finishing my gymnastics training, I inherently knew the accuracy in this as soon as I heard it.

And that opening scene, well... to tidy it up... I ended up staying on the farm to complete the program the full twelve weeks. I moved into a transition granny flat in a small local coastal town. There I swam with dolphins, read and thought more about what I might like to do with my future. Though the option is open for most to stay on longer if they felt they needed it, the staff got wind of the developing sexual relationship between Warwick and me. They reminded us we were breaking the rules and one or both of us would have to leave. Given I had only ever planned three months, and that Warwick's court case depended upon him staying on the farm for a reduced sentence, I left. I moved into a transition house and to continue with outreach counselling to assist me in keeping on track.

Our relationship continued with our altered living arrangements, though both of us had deep-seated trust issues with the other. This created some angst and arguably distraction from our own rehabilitation. Though it could also be said it helped provide more 'food for therapy' through the 'mirroring' capacity of partnership. We both remained drug, including alcohol-free for six months, with Warwick leaving the farm and living back south of the river with his mum on a suspended sentence. Warwick ended up drinking some alcohol on a friend's birthday, which led to us drinking together a couple of days later. This led to a weakened ability to say no, and a morphing of our resolve. It is said you only have so many 'no's' available before you end up saying 'yes'. That's why it is recommended you change your friend group, and anything else associated with the drug or people still using.

All you hear about picking straight back up where you left off when you relapse with a drug you have abused is true. I jumped straight back in like a fish feeding frenzy after being 'clean' for just over ten months. Warwick plummeted to the dregs he'd risen from too. We started dealing with the second 'score' after coming out of rehab. We used connections we'd made through recovery to get drugs. If I thought my car had been carrying enough drugs to jail me for a long time with Steve, I was probably kidding myself. Now I was looking at spending most of my adult life behind bars should we get caught. I learned Warwick was a pig with drugs. He shot up way more than he could handle and expected me to 'bring' him back when that included heroin. So rather than enjoy the languorous high 'H' would provide after the hectic pace of amphetamines, I would spend my supposed 'coming downtime', dragging him blueberry-faced into a cold shower. I'd slap him across the face, beating his chest and when it really got bad, calling the ambulance to resuscitate him. For someone so good at using, he was bloody ridiculous with figuring out how much smack he could handle - though mysteriously good with what I could.

So, our relationship soured pretty quickly with our extreme sport of choice 'drug use' back in the picture. It was almost as if we were trying to prove how 'good' at using we could be to the other. In the harsh reality of what we were like, I feel for Warwick's poor mother, in whose house we spent most of our time. Her bedroom was right next to Warwick's. She dealt with our erratic comings and goings and the incessant arguments. There was also the raiding of her fridge and Warwick's escalating disrespect at the same rate of increased drug use. She must have known the nightmare that was going on. Having lived it before, it must have almost killed her. She probably didn't get much sleep either.

Before that initial scene of us circling one another like vultures, we hadn't slept for two weeks. To say drugs deluded us is probably an understatement. We heard the carpet and walls talking to us. And we swore there was a fed's camera in the light bulb which we had to keep on rather than be in the dark. At some point we were too scared to even leave the room to go to the toilet, we were that paranoid. It was probably the scariest, darkest, 'lit up' place in my life within the four corners of that room. It petrified me into absolute motionlessness.

After that scene in the Jacaranda lined streets of Applecross in the middle-class southern suburb of Perth, Warwick and I broke up. I got clean the second and final time at my parents' home through yoga, meditation, will power and as an outpatient with the counsellors from the farm at their city office. About six months after we separated, I heard Warwick died of a heroin overdose and I couldn't help but feel it would have been different if I was there to resuscitate him. I was saddened, but not surprised. I had thought that would happen unless he stopped using. He just could never figure out how much he needed to use to come down. Or maybe he did.

Chapter Two

FINDING MY WAY HOME TO TRUTH

Satya

Playlist - Thompson Twins, Lies 1983

At seven, I learned to Lie. It was like one day I woke up, discovered a new trick and decided I'd explore it in as many ways as I could. I went through a stage where I swear every second sentence that came out of my mouth was not the truth. I told white lies and massive big dirty lies. I withheld the truth, stretched the truth, offered bald-faced lies and bold-faced lies, lying through my teeth, and lying by complete fabrication. There are apparently twenty-eight ways to lie. I'm sure I gave time to each of them, practiced them all, except for those that relate to trading, I'm not sure I did that at seven.

"My uncle's Elton John," I told a classmate. (He **definitely** was **not**. I don't even know why I said he was. Why would anyone want Elton John to be their uncle anyway?)

"I didn't do it, Melanie did," I told my mum when I was the culprit who'd eaten the last biscuit even when we were clearly told not to.

"Melanie did it," I told my mum when I accidentally broke the chair.

"It's Melanie's fault," I told my mum about why we were late home from the park.

"I forgot my lunch," to the canteen lady when I didn't want to eat the vegemite sandwich I'd asked my mum for, to eat for lunch.

My mum, who was aware of what I was doing, tried everything to get me to stop, even fabrication and storytelling herself.

"Your nose will continue to grow like Pinocchio's," she threatened and "the reason for that pimple on your tongue is from all the lying you've been doing."

But I didn't pay much attention, even though I was discovering the difficulty of maintaining a lie. How much work it took trying to remember the right 'story' and which 'story' you gave to whom. Eventually, it came to pass that I told the Lie to end all lies, well most anyway.

I went to a local small school not far from where we lived, and I walked there daily. The suburb I lived in was a growing community of hard-working families who'd battled to get their foot in on the Great Australian Dream, owning their own homes. It was the year that Malcolm Fraser was Prime Minister and the majestic story of love between humans and feathered friends in the film 'Storm boy' came out. We had just got a coloured tv.

I was in a mixed year class of thirty or so and fell in the older age range. My teacher, Miss Wilson, was a young and beautiful lady of about twenty-four with the fashionable hairdo of the time, dead-straight hair, with a blunt short fringe. She wore long, flowing dresses and skirts, and loved to play guitar. She was timid for a teacher - almost placid - and we ran circles around her - nicely. I was a diligent, naturally intelligent and inquisitive student, with an active imagination. I was polite, quiet, and caring. 'That' student to bring the apple to the teacher or give the tissues when she was crying. Always looking for ways to help and assist, struggling with both wanting to be 'seen' while simultaneously 'hiding' chameleon-like in amongst my peers.

We were in the middle of a pretty (uninteresting) boring maths lesson when over the PA the principal made an announcement.

"This is a special announcement for all students and teachers. All classes, please follow your teachers' instruction and to make your way to the undercover area for an emergency assembly in ten minutes," Principle Lambert announced.

I turned my head and raised my eyebrows at my best friend, Tania. Tania was about the same height and build as me, just a bit taller. Together we were the second and third smallest in the class for our year. She was very knowledgeable and sometimes outspoken, though most of the time quiet like me. She and her mum always seemed to know what was going on with everyone. Tania shrugged her shoulders and raised her eyebrows back, with a certain glint in her eye.

"Children, please make your way to the toilet if you need to go quickly so we can prepare ourselves for the Special Assembly. Leave your books where they are, we can pick this back up again when we return," said Miss Wilson in her soft musical voice.

I nodded to Tania in the toilet's direction. She nodded in agreement.

Tania and I, along with as a couple of other boys and girls, made our way to the toilet block, very close to our classroom.

"I wonder what it's all about Tania?" I asked, over the twinkling, splashing and swishing of urination flowing into the bowl.

"Yeah me too," she said. Then in a conspiring tone, "You know I saw Ana-Nicole, the year seven, up at the office at morning tea crying, with her mum. Maybe it's something to do with that?"

This was news to me. I wasn't aware of Ana-Nicole crying, and I began to wonder what she might have been crying about. I heard the toilet flush in the booth next door.

"C'mon, hurry up, let's go," said Tania, probably realising I was now sitting digesting the information she'd just given me.

We made our way back to the classroom. The bulk of the class was forming a line in preparation to walk in as much an orderly fashion that six- and seven-year-olds can muster. Then we headed to the undercover area with the entire school.

There was an air of excitement as our class line approached the school assembly area. This was an unusual event and a break from the 'Groundhog Day' monotony a school day can deliver.

"Ahm, Ahum" began the school principal, clearing his throat as he stood at the front of the ever-forming audience of children. "Please make your way in an **orderly** and **quiet** fashion children, seating yourselves down **quickly**."

Without too much pushing or shoving, the five hundred or so of us made our way to sit on the cold concrete. Mr Lambert, standing in baby blue knee-length shorts, shushed us, and motioned with his hands for us to be quiet and seated. He re-arranged his attire, pulling his matching socks up to just under the knee, checked the microphone's height and then began, as we waited with anticipation.

"Good afternoon, children," said Mr Lambert.

"Good afternoon Mr Lambert," we returned in a chorus-like fashion.

"Okay, so if we can just maintain that silence now, thank you, I will not be taking up much of your time. I have called this special assembly as something happened yesterday after school we need to share with you all, to keep you from danger."

Tania and I shared an intrigued look with one another, me raising both eyebrows, Tania just the one. I always thought she was so smart to be able to do this, and on those times I tried to raise one eyebrow too, we ended in fits of laughter. While the principal was conducting an assembly was not the best time for me to attempt this.

Besides something much greater was unfolding.

The electricity and excitement in the room tingled.

"A man in a white van approached one of our older students as she was walking home from school," stated Mr Lambert in a matter of a fact tone.

I felt Tania's eyes darting towards mine, capturing my gaze. Eyebrow raised.

"The man asked the girl if she would like a lift home."

"Ana- Nicole," Tania whispered to me. "I bet."

"And the girl ignored the man who she didn't know and continued to walk faster toward her home."

"Wow," I wide-eyed mouthed at Tania.

"Another car luckily came along, and the man in the white van sped off."

"After some discussion with the police this morning, and the girl and the family involved, we decided it was in the best interest of all students that we share this information. You will be each taking a note home this evening so your parents are aware of the situation," Mr Lambert said.

He gazed around at the five hundred dumbstruck students. Nothing like this ever happened in the sleepy little suburb of Greenwood.

I glanced at Tania, who was looking all-important like she knew about this way before they told us.

"We ask that if someone approaches you, you do as the senior student did. Remember the rules of Stranger Danger. Your teachers will go over this with you this afternoon to make sure you all know what to do if anyone you do not know stops you. Just as the senior student did, you must ignore the person and continue walking toward your home or where more people are, whichever is closest. **Do not get into the car with anyone you do not know ever unless you have direct permission from your parents or some other authority figure**. I will repeat that. **Do not get into any car, with anyone you do not know, ever, unless you have permission from your parents or some other person of authority**," Mr Lambert sternly warned us all.

"The police have also asked if anyone has any other information on this or has been approached by a man in a van. If you know anything else, please let us or them know as soon as possible. They are working on this case now, and there have been other sightings and similar experiences at schools around the area. So, if this has happened to you, or to anyone you know, please let your teachers know as soon as you go back to the classroom. That is all. School dismissed. Assembly finished, please listen to your teachers for further instruction and make your way back to your classroom quietly in an orderly fashion."

"Good afternoon, children," Mr Lambert finalised the assembly.

"Good afternoon Mr Lambert," we parrot-fashioned back.

And at that point, something inside happened. As the stunned hum of quiet voices between friends began, and we formed a line, nudging, jostling and standing tall with knowing glances, a story within me began to grow and unfold.

We made our way back one by one, class by class, each to our appointed classrooms. My mind began to create, to weave, as my body started to jitter at the immensity of what I was about to propose. Tania poked me in the back with her finger and tried to get me to turn around, but I wouldn't. I was too immersed in the Bigness of what I was thinking.

We made our way past the sparkling sunny courtyard with its pegged up year-old plants and blossoming flowers towards the bright poster-covered interior of our classroom. Then we each found our seats amid the cold hard plastic.

"Quiet now children, let's get back to our seats as quickly as we can. I would like to add something to what Mr Lambert has shared before we get back to our maths lesson," said Miss Wilson in her quiet, melodious voice.

We quickly made our way back to our seats, hungry for more information on the most significant thing to happen since 'In the Wild' with Harry Butler started on colour TV.

"Okay, so first, I would like to talk to you about stranger danger. Now, what do we remember about stranger danger? Can anyone tell me anything? Please put your hand up and tell me what you know."

Four or five of the older students put their hands up, my bestie included, indicating they had a response. Tania looked like she was bursting as she put her hand STRAIGHT up into the air. Left armpit way beyond her nose, she used her right hand to assist her in thrusting it up even higher.

"Yes, Tania," allowed Miss Wilson.

"It's about when someone you don't know asks you something. Like a man asks you if you want a lift and you don't know him," Tania said with quiet confidence.

"That's right Tania," conceded Miss Wilson. "And if a man or woman approached us from a car we **didn't** know as we were walking to or from school, or in fact anytime, what would we do?"

"Ignore him," a boy yelled from the back.

"Tell him no way," said another close to him.

"Yeah, tell him to get stuffed," said Craig, the scruffy boy who was always fighting.

"Okay, okay enough, enough. Hands, **please**. We answer in an orderly fashion," implored Miss Wilson. "They are ALL right answers, though. Possibly better just to ignore them though rather than trying to have some conversation with them. Then what would we do? Hands only please."

I raised my hand in amongst a sea of others.

"Yes Mandi."

Here was my moment. I swallowed before I spoke. I noticed my palms felt a little clammy. "Miss Wilson we would have to walk off, quickly. Like I did."

"Yes, that's right… hold on… Like you did, Mandi?" asked Miss Wilson gently and precariously.

"Y-yes," I responded.

"When did this happen, Mandi?"

I took another deep breath as I felt my heartbeat quicken, and my mouth goes dry. "Just this morning, Miss Wilson, as I was walking to school."

My beloved teacher looked at me with alarm.

"Okay class, I would like you to continue working through your maths books. Mandi, I would like you to please come outside."

As I got up from my chair, I felt the weight of the class's eyes on me. The drama and excitement were getting even better!

Tania tried to get my attention frantically, non-verbally. She was having difficulty trying to figure out what was going on.

Although it was only about three metres to the door, it felt like time was both speeding up and slowing down at the same time.

Just outside the door, Miss Wilson asked me to tell her exactly what had happened.

On the spot, I verbalised my 'story' for the first time.

"WWWell, Miss Wilson, this morning as I was walking to school a man in a van stopped, and I just ran off away from him." As I spoke, I moved from foot to foot, trying to look earnest and truthful.

"Okay, Mandi, that must have been scary for you. Do you remember what colour the van was?" Miss Wilson tried to coax from me.

I covered my face with my hand. "Um, I think maybe it was white?"

Miss Wilson adjusted her gaze and looked me straight in the eye which was difficult because it is not where I wanted to look at her. "And do you remember what the man looked like?"

"Not really, Miss Wilson, but he was ugly and scary, like a monster which is why I got scared and ran." I tried to sound as honest as I could.

"Hmm," Miss Wilson said earnestly. "I think you'd better tell Mr Lambert about this, so you both can tell the police."

All of a sudden, my 'story' didn't seem like so much fun anymore, but it was too late to back out from it. Even though my legs were feeling a little shaky, I found a voice and said a small tiny, "Okay." I wasn't sure if Miss Wilson believed me. Part of me thought she might have, part of me felt she didn't. Now it seemed this story was bigger than me. I wished I hadn't opened my mouth. She wrote a note for me to pass to the headmaster and put it in a closed envelope.

"Mandi, give this to Mrs Timtley at the office when you get there. She will give it to Mr Lambert," Miss Wilson said.

She gently touched my arm.

"It will be okay, just tell the truth."

I was incapable of speaking and just nodded instead. As I walked away from my classroom with the envelope in my hand, it felt as though my world was shifting. It felt dreamlike, though not a sweet dream, a bit of a scary dream, maybe even a nightmare. I felt like I was walking away from my old life, and I wasn't sure what the new one would look like. I held the envelope up to the sun. I looked to see if I could open it to see what she wrote. No such luck. I continued to the headmaster. My date with Destiny.

With much courage, I pushed open the glass door to the school office. Mrs Timtley, an older woman with big glasses, glanced up from her pile of paperwork and peered at me, asking, "And what, young lady, can I do for you?"

"Um, I'm here to see Principal Lambert," I muttered as I passed her the precarious envelope.

"Okay, and your name and class?" she asked.

"Mandi, Mandi Nelson. Miss Wilson's class."

"Just a moment and I will let him know. Please take a seat there."

She pointed towards the naughty bench. I had never sat on the naughty bench. It was a seat passers-by outside could see. It meant I was in Trouble. And if **anyone** went passed, they would see. The whole world would know. This was enough for me to resolve to make my story so much better so Mr Lambert would definitely believe me. I couldn't be seen on the naughty bench. I wasn't a naughty child.

Mrs Timtley broke me out of my reverie by stepping out of the principal's office, allowing just a little of Mr Lambert's desk to be seen.

"Principal Lambert will see you now," said Mrs Timtley.

With knees knocking, pulse-quickening, hands pooling sweat upon the palms, I gathered together all the muster and courage I could summon. I pulled my shoulders back like Nanny had shown me with balanced books on my head and made my way towards the daunting doorway and what lay within.

"Enter Mandi Nelson," Mr Lambert's voice boomed.

"Thank you, Principal Lambert," I shakily responded.

"Stand," he motioned with his large hands towards the opposite side of the desk from him.

He was sitting behind an imposing desk with neat piles of paperwork, and a silver-framed picture of his family with a filing cabinet to his left. Mounted behind him, a threatening image of a lion about to pounce on a zebra. His office smelled of leather and furniture polish. It was the first time I had ever been to Mr Lambert's office, and suddenly, the task that lay ahead daunted me.

I stood quietly as Mr Lambert read the note I'd brought. He rubbed his fingers on his thumb as he understood what Miss Wilson had written, then started to stroke his chin. I could smell his aftershave. He put the note down and placed both hands under his chin. His gaze firmly fixed upon me.

"Mandi, I would like you to know that this matter is a very ser-i-ous matter."

He was enunciating his words slowly, making sure I didn't miss a thing.

"It is a dangerous situation where somebody could get hurt. It is **very important** that you tell me the truth, that you tell me as much as you can remember, little bit by little bit, okay?"

I nodded, okay. I thought maybe he might believe me. He's asking for a little bit by little bit.

"Would you like to tell me about what happened this morning on your way to school?" he asked.

I took a really, really deep breath, and pushed my shoulders back. "Well, you see Mr Lambert," I began with a false confidence, "I was just walking to school like I usually do."

"Hmm," said Mr Lambert. "Yes, I see you live in Elm Way, Right okay."

"And as I was walking a man in a van stopped and said, "Get in." (I put on a gruff voice.) "And I just ran off away from him," I said as I moved from foot to foot, trying to look as earnestly, wide-eyed as possible.

"Hmm" said Mr Lambert. "And do you remember what the van looked like?"

"Yes, it was white," I said, believing my story more as I told it the second time.

"And what did the man look like?"

"He was big and ugly like a monster," I repeated.

"And was anyone else with you?"

"Yes," I said in a moment that changed all forever, "Tania."

"Tania Geecross? OK well then, I would like you to get her from the class too."

"Now?" I asked.

"Yes, please Mandi," said Mr Lambert. "We will get your account of events then phone the police to have them come down to take your statement. It's **very** important we get these details right."

I slunk out of the room and the school office uncertain of how I would get Tania to go along with me. I arrived back at our classroom and knocked on the door, interrupting Miss Wilson from her resumed maths session, asking for Tania to be excused to see Mr Lambert too.

Tania made her way outside to meet me, one raised eyebrow after another, curiosity overwhelming her. As soon as we were out of ear-shot, she grabbed both of my hands and whirled me around to face her.

"Mandi, what is going on?"

"You have to come with me and say you were walking with me this morning. Tell them you saw the man too in the van," I implored, letting go of one hand and dragging her with the other.

"But I didn't," said Tania.

She let go of my hand.

"And how could we have walked together when we don't even live next to each other?" she rightfully asked.

My heart began to sink. In my haste to grab a collaborator to make my story the truth, I had forgotten a significant sticking point. Tania couldn't have been with me this morning because we didn't even live near one another.

I grabbed at straws as I could feel myself sinking, and the office was getting closer. "We could say that you slept at my place the night."

"But Mandi," Tania said. "I didn't."

I was sinking; the ground was sinking. The earth was shifting, and I was going under, way, way under. 'Maybe to never return' under. I became desperate.

"Please, Tania," I begged as we approached the door to the school office. "Please," I mouthed as we walked in.

Tania didn't respond. She kept walking, undaunted by the naughty bench which she didn't have to sit on, unafraid of the desk, nor even Mr Lambert, the headmaster. Confidently, she made her way to stand on the opposite side of Mr Lambert, and I made my way beside her.

"Hello Tania. Thank you for coming into the office. So, Mandi tells me you were with her this morning and that you were both stopped by a white van."

"Hello, Mr Lambert," said Tania.

I held my breath. Time stopped. I waited to hear what she would say with never felt before baited anticipation.

She didn't say anything for a while and moved from foot to foot, perhaps deliberating her friendship with me, versus the truth.

"Tania," Mr Lambert said. "Were you with Mandi this morning? I see you live at opposite ends of Greenacre."

Tania shot a conciliatory, apologetic look at me, then responded. "No, I wasn't."

I felt like a balloon that lost all of its air. The impending weight of my lie was about to come earthing down upon me, and I was sick to my stomach.

"Okay," said Mr Lambert. "So, you were not with Mandi this morning, Tania?"

"No," repeated Tania as I sunk deeper into the bowels of the earth.

"Okay, Mandi, you have some explaining to do," said Mr Lambert.

It was impossible for me to speak. It was impossible for me even to lift my downcast eyes to meet Mr Lambert's. My whole world had just shifted, and I didn't know what I should say or do. I had forgotten how to tell the truth. I was just trying to rapidly find my way out of this with another lie.

"Anything to say, Mandi?" Mr Lambert prompted.

"She wasn't with me, Mr Lambert," I managed. Might as well get her off the hook. "But everything else still happened."

"Hmm," he said as he tapped a pen upon his desk. "I would like to share a story with you. Tania you can stay to hear it. Then we might think about what happened this morning."

Mr Lambert told us Aesop's fable about 'The Boy who called Wolf.' The general gist of this story is that a bored shepherd boy who looks after sheep goes running to the village crying out wolf when there is none. When the villagers arrive, he laughs at their stupidity. He does this twice, then when on the third time an actual wolf comes, he runs to warn the villagers. No one believes him, and they lose many sheep.

I allowed this story to settle with me and shame burned brightly brandishing through my heart and my lies.

"Mandi, do you understand why I have shared this story with you?" Mr Lambert asked gently.

"Yes, Mr Lambert," I said. "If I lie about it, then it really happens, maybe no one will pay any attention."

"Yes, that's right," said Mr Lambert. "The truth will always set you free."

The magnitude of those words settled in and around me. They felt comforting.

"I'm sorry, Mr Lambert," I managed in a tiny voice.

"I think we've learned an important lesson here," Mr Lambert kindly offered. "Now, did anything out of the ordinary happen this morning Mandi?"

"No, Mr Lambert," I quietly conceded, holding the tears back.

"Okay, well I would like you to remember this lesson Mandi, and you too Tania. It will serve you in good stead in your lives. Both dismissed now, please go back to the classroom."

Tania and I left the room together, making our way past the naughty seat and Mrs Timtley, out through the glass door.

I turned to Tania, with tears in my eyes and said, "I'm so sorry, Tania."

She grabbed my hand in hers and turned to me and tenderly kissed my cheek.

"It's okay you silly rascal," she said.

Together we made our way back to the class. I felt relief, and like I'd just faced my biggest fear, and it had all turned out okay. Shame and guilt still burned a little through me, but I had a clear sense of it all being okay.

But that was it, a definite turning point for me, the Great Lie to end **all** lies. Well, almost. It signalled a move for me towards honesty, closing the door on deception as I made a conscious effort to speak with more Truth. And a big word for a seven-year-old, towards more integrity, though it was still a long way to go yet.

This experience led to the 'truth' being something that burned brightly within, a quality I held close to my heart because I learned it the hard way. I learned what it was like to live in the space of untruth, to fester in fabrication, the internal dissonance created in dishonesty. Through my exploration of lies, tales, distortion and diversion, I learned about the energy it took to maintain a lie or a 'story.' And I learned about the effect it had on my personal relationships and my inner harmony. I discovered the knock-on effect of the shame and guilt and that feeling within of deep uncomfortableness and the forever concern of being 'caught' or 'found' out.

Yoga's second Yama 'Satya' in its purest form, calls for the devotee to cultivate truthfulness, to think, speak and act with integrity, and this experience marked the beginning of refinement in that area.

Chapter Three

TAKING WHAT WASN'T MINE

Asteya

Playlist - Jane's Addiction - Been Caught Stealing 1990

A lot happened the year I turned seven and was in Miss Wilson's class. It was a **big** year for me on many levels. On a spiritual level, we are completing our first seven-year cycle of growth, learning to live upon the Earth. We were grounding ourselves, building our immune system and our energy shell or aura. It is the experiences of these first seven years that apparently help to make the foundation of the future life we want to build. In particular, the age of seven is right in between what the 'learning mind' (https://www.learning-mind.com/7-chakra-life-cycles-and-crisis-years/) refers to as the crisis years. We then enter the turning point of seven to fourteen, moving more into the sexual realm of discovery. A time of identifying with gender roles and exploring the world outside of our family through sports and extra-curricular activities. It was also while

I was seven that I began to explore the 3rd Yama, 'Asteya - non-stealing' in the 'simplest' of ways.

***

There was a boy we all seemed to like. Dean was new to the school. With straight blond hair and blue eyes, he was slightly bigger than the other boys, having stayed down a year, and popular with all the girls. Tania and I both liked him, but so did Nadia and Tammy. When we did our music lesson, we all hustled and jostled to sit near him.

It was a smelly, wet-armpit afternoon, and we'd just come in from lunch. I was feeling a little tired as I made my way with Tania back into the classroom. We'd been playing with the skipping ropes, and it was unusually warm weather for Perth in late April.

"Children, don't get too comfortable, you don't need anything from your desk right now. Just pack away everything from your desk and we will begin to make our way quietly to the music room," suggested Miss Wilson.

We hastily, gleefully did as she asked then formed a line of boys and girls in preparation. Without incident, we marched the short distance, then found space on the carpet in the instrument lined walls of the music room. While Miss Wilson was setting up the cassette player, we jostled for space with one another upon the green and yellow weaved carpet.

"Quietly and quickly remember people. Just find a space, there is plenty of room," Miss Wilson reminded.

Dean beckoned to Tania and me. He had a spot near the back of the room, to the side. We made our way to sit either side of Dean, getting there before Tammy and Nadia. It was always a 'thing' to sit next to Dean, and the two sets of friends were forever trying to get there first.

"Hi Tania," said Dean looking towards his right. "Hi Mandi," he said, looking towards his left. We share smiles all around.

"Shh," Miss Wilson reminded. "Let's all quiet down now. Find a comfortable spot now with your legs crossed or extended. I would like you to close your eyes."

Miss Wilson dimmed the lights. From the cassette player, which connected to a speaker system, some beautiful melodious music began to play.

"We will listen to the music, and I would like you to notice where your mind goes, to just relax," Miss Wilson instructed.

It wasn't long before I felt Dean's hand reach across for mine. I peeked and noticed he'd reached for Tania's too. His hand was warm and a little sweaty with little callouses on the pads of his palms. They felt so boyish. The gentle music continued, and I tried to allow my mind to drift, but I was super conscious of my hand in Dean's. I felt him release my hand and move his way down my thigh, lifting my skirt a little and placing his hand and fingers over my cotton butterfly knickers. It felt nice, and I noticed a warmness in my groin. I peeked, and it didn't seem he was doing this to Tania. It made me feel special. Chosen. He held his hand there moving it just a little, and my face burned. I was finding it impossible to concentrate on the music.

I wondered if Miss Wilson could see what was happening, so I opened my eyes momentarily and was assured from where she was sitting, she couldn't see. I couldn't look at Dean. The room smelled of sweat and moist underwear. After a while, Dean moved his hand from my pants and slowly placed my hand back in his, guiding my hand to his shorts. My breath caught in my throat. His 'thing' seemed to poke up a bit, and it felt weird for me, so I moved my hand away.

Nothing happened after that. As strangely as this had begun it stopped, like a flash of an unidentified object breaking through some stargazing on a clear night sky. Then disappearing, into nothingness, leaving you feeling a little disturbed and wondering. For me, anyway. When I opened my eyes again, I saw Dean was making his way to Tania's pants. I closed my eyes, squeezed them tight and kept them shut. Not wanting to see anymore, I tried to listen to the music. To let go of what I had felt and seen. I wanted to forget what happened and what might be happening between Tania and Dean. I could smell that moist, sweaty, urine smell even more.

Tania and I didn't talk about what happened that day, ever, in fact.

The next day, I arrived at school at my usual time, always a little later than Tania but about ten minutes before the bell went. Tania came rushing up to me eager to show me something.

"Mandi, have a look at this," she said, opening a ring box.

Inside was a gold diamond ring with three massive stones. (Or what looked like a diamond ring. It was probably diamantes).

"Oh wow," I exclaimed. "Where did you get that?"

"Dean gave it to me this morning," she proudly replied. "I think it's three diamonds. I'll have to get my mum to check it."

My heart sunk. Even though I didn't want to do what it seemed Dean wanted me to do yesterday, it didn't mean I didn't like him. I still had feelings for him. And now it seemed he liked Tania and only Tania.

That day at school, where one part of me eagerly waited for Dean to gift me too, the other part knew that this wasn't going to happen. I thought about things and figured perhaps if I gave Dean something extraordinary, he might like me again. What did I have at home? Our house wasn't as lavish as Tania's, or now *it seemed* Dean's. I knew there weren't any diamond rings lying around, and I also knew I couldn't ask my mum to buy a present for Dean. She was always going on about money. I kept thinking all day about what I might give Dean.

When I got home, I searched for something as good or better than the diamond ring Dean gave Tania. I searched my room thinking of perhaps giving him my favourite soft toy, but this didn't seem like the right gift. Although special to me, I didn't think it would be special to Dean. I searched in my mum's wooden jewellery box while she wasn't looking, but there wasn't much in there. Most of it was too girly, and silver, not gold like Tania's ring. I searched in my dad's drawers and found nothing in there either. Just socks and jocks and blue work singlets.

I'd almost given up, but later that night when I was brushing my teeth, I thought about searching the bathroom cupboards. Lo-and-behold I found a spectacular prize. I was so excited I almost spat the toothpaste out on the bathroom cabinet and not in the sink. A sparkly man's gold ring. "Oh my," I thought, with my eyes almost popping out of my head. "The absolute perfect gift. This will win back Dean." I found some wrapping paper and wrapped the gift. Momentarily I stopped and felt a little tinge of guilt to think perhaps it might be my dad's wedding ring.

It was difficult to sleep that night. Excitement and guilt consumed me. The next day I prepared myself and arrived at school at a much earlier time than usual. I put my bag down and tried to find Dean. I saw him on the oval kicking the footy with some other boys. I went up to him.

"Hi Dean," I said shyly.

"Oh, hi Mandi," he said nonchalantly.

"I have a present for you," I said as I produced the prized wrapped ring from my pocket.

Dean didn't say thank you, just snatched it from my hands, opened it and said, "Right okay, great," put it in his pocket and ran off to mark the football.

And I waited. And waited. And waited.

Lucky I wasn't holding my breath because he never spoke to me of it again. He didn't thank me. He didn't acknowledge it beyond putting it in his pocket on the oval. Needless to say, the ring didn't change anything between us. He remained Tania's boyfriend. Nothing ever happened between us again. I stopped liking him so much too, for not appreciating I'd given him my dad's ring.

Meanwhile, for me, as time went by I became wracked with guilt, and even more so when a couple of months later, my dad declared he had lost his wedding ring. I felt absolutely sick with remorse and guilt but was still in my 'lying' stage so I couldn't find the words or the courage to tell him I'd taken it. He ended up buying a new one.

These feelings of shame stayed with me until I was about twenty-four or twenty-five when I finally had the nerve to hold a conversation with my dad about it. On some level, I understood that subconsciously holding onto this was probably affecting my behaviour.

"Dad, I have something to tell you that I should have told you years ago, but didn't have the courage too," I said.

"Right," my dad responded as he raised his bushy eyebrows. "Go on then."

"You know how you lost your wedding ring all those years ago?" I paused and Dad nodded his head. "I took it from the bathroom cupboard and gave it to a boy in my class." That was it. The truth was out.

"Oh, right." He smiled. "That wasn't my ring. I found that on a job."

"But I remember you said you'd lost your ring? It was around the same time I took it," I stated. I was feeling confused.

"Yeah, I lost it in the ocean. I always used to take it off to go for a swim because it was slightly too big." He started to laugh. "So, you've been carrying that for how long?" he managed between laughter.

"Almost eighteen years."

Chapter Four

PATH TO PURITY AND RIGHT USE OF ENERGY

Brahmacharya

Playlist - Stairway to Heaven - Led Zeppelin, 1971

There are many other ways to view Asteya, the third Yama of Patanjali's pathway to a yogi. One we often don't think about so much is *not stealing from ourselves*. Until I became *dedicated* to my practice and my growth. I was the thief to myself. I took the life I was born to live, by living in my untruth. I ignored the whisperings of my soul and dialled up the familiar noise of the masses, which did not suit me well. I'm not sure it suits anyone well. I continued to fool myself seeking outside assistance to help me understand why I was so unhappy when I was 'living the dream'. In the latter 2000s, I was following the rules, making good money, in a 'mature' relationship, with two healthy kids, driving a convertible, living in one of the most desirable places in the world.

Yet still, something was not quite there. Drinking too much at decadent lunches, too much on the weekend, on a Friday. Getting caught drink driving, not once or twice but three times over the space of decades. Enlisting the help of psychologists to help figure out what is going on, being so numb to my inner voice that it had been pushed beyond mute. We all know the story, and inherently know it's the system that's flawed not us. Many of us are in a job we despise yet are caught in to pay the rent or mortgage. We wake every Monday next to a partner we stopped loving years ago because you stopped growing together. 'Sticking' it out for the kids' sake, dreading the week ahead. Counting the days to the weekend so you can have a couple of glasses of wine on Friday; enough to find some 'freedom' in amongst all the chained obligation. We all know the story because most of us live it. It takes courage and indomitable strength to swim against the incoming tide.

"Swim, Dory, swim," my fourteen-billion-years old spirit whispered.

In the Yamas and Niyamas of Patanjali's sutras, one meanders gracefully into another so the lines between the two become blurred. From non- stealing, we move into refinement. So that Divine spark within me, carrying all the Ancient wisdom of those who lived before, beckoned me to stop stealing from myself and to start 'polishing' the truth of who I was. In traditional yogic terms, this was referred to as Bramachyra, celibacy or the right use of energy. For me, I also see Bramachyra as linked with the Niyama, Saucha, the Sanskrit word for purity or cleanliness. In the Western yogic world, Bramachyra has been referred to as meaning 'moderation of the senses', and I, for the most part, view this as a western cop-out. An inability to walk the 'true' yogic path as perhaps it required more discipline than most could muster.

Sri Swami Sivananda in the 'Practice of Brahmacharya' (1934) says:

"Brahmacharya is the vow of celibacy. The term 'celibacy' is from the Latin 'caelebs,' meaning unmarried or single, and signifies the state of living unmarried. Abode of supreme peace begins from Brahmacharya or purity… Brahmacharya is absolute freedom from sexual desires and thoughts. A real Brahmachara will not feel any difference in touching a woman, a piece of paper, or a block of wood. Brahmacharya is meant for both men and women."

Being an extremist, I allowed the pendulum to swing equally in both directions.

In October 2008, I was living in wine capital, sleepy, except for international surf competition time, Leeuwin Estate Concert Weekends, and let's face it all other school holiday and public holidays, iconic Margaret River. The GFC (Global Financial Crisis) had hit a year ago. I'd had to let go of my cushy, lucrative real estate job, and I was volunteering at a not for profit child sexual abuse foundation while I rethought my next career plans. Earlier that year I'd undertaken a weekend film course with internationally known Richard Todd, of movie 'Frackman' renown. I'd picked up where I had left my dreams as a teenager and young adult, following my grandfather Bill's footsteps, with a love of media.

Before the GFC, the local paper interviewed me for the real estate section, like a 'get to know….' story. They asked me what I would do if I weren't doing real estate. I answered I'd be making films about people's lives. I was taking a reprieve from 'life' as I pondered how to make this happen, and also waiting with everything crossed for some of my outstanding sales commissions to settle.

The Monday directly following the course had all of my creative juices over-flowing, and this was what was to become the foundation of 'CherishYOU'. I contacted my maternal grandparents who lived three and a half hours away and asked them if I could go there on that day to film them in conversation. I had a unique and close relationship with Huey and Ivy, as they had bought me up for the first couple of years of my life. My parents dropped me to stay with my grandmother early in the morning while they, and separately, my grandfather, went to work, and then we all ate dinner together, before heading home to sleep. The next day to wake up and do it all over again. I was blessed to share a unique and coveted bond with Huey and Ivy, and they were the first to teach and offer me unconditional love.

As they'd aged and repeated themselves more, I realised I was no longer listening to them. I was zoning out. I was no longer communicating with my grandparents. I had checked out of the relationship. An epiphany hit as a result of the film course; that I could capture footage of immense meaning for others and the first people I thought to capture was my beloved grandparents. For no other reason than they were both in their 80s at the time and therefore probably close to moving on from this life, I was keen to capture some of their wisdom for my children and my children's children. Which was pretty funny because I didn't even own a camera, video nor DSLR. As soon as they agreed I raced around town to find a video camera I could use. And of course, I did, because I'm sure Spirit was playing a part in this.

I drove to Perth, amidst a 'sprinkly' day, roof off. Rain only hits you when the car stops for traffic lights, and there weren't too many lights between Marg's and Bunbury, alternating with Black-eyed Peas, Sarah Blasko and Kings of Leon. I filmed my cherished grandparents in conversation about important life moments for three hours, camera set up hoisted up on books. It was rough going that first time. Then I turned around and drove three and a half hours home.

I recall getting back at 9pm, pouring myself a glass of local red wine, feeling really tired yet incredible satiated. And pretty much in awe I'd answered a calling, a deep service for not only my grandparents but for humanity. It felt extraordinary. I knew the rest of the large extended family would love it, and my grandparents appreciated my honouring of them. I felt I'd done something of value. I sat with the footage for months, unable to touch it, to begin editing as I had the feeling as soon as I started it, either Huey or Ivy would die.

I got an itch to begin the editing process mid-September, almost a year later, and things simultaneously started to decline for my grandfather. I completed the editing, and he passed in early October in hospital having just turned ninety. Although he'd lived a full life with ample time upon the planet, it was still a problematic death to deal with. He and my grandmother formed the pinnacle of my mum's family. It was a much closer family bond for me than my dad's and contributed to a beautiful experience of familial love with all the extended relatives. It was the end of an era. Disconnected from my truth and centre; I didn't know how to deal with it authentically. Many years before I experienced death, including a close cousin, best friend and past lover, and associates dying in the years proceeding. My grandfather, Hubert Brown-Neaves, a decade and a half later, was the closest person to me who'd died who I'd known my entire life.

So, I coped in the manner I handled everything else until that point, in the way I'd utilised for many years, escapism. I drank. Not daily, 'in-the-mornings' style drinking but definitely most evenings in the lead up to his funeral. I polished off between a half and a full bottle of red wine while I edited. And alcohol magnificently brings up all we are yet to deal with. It gets the record caught and stuck on repeat in the groove. It allows the mind to loop continuously, to be captured in all sorts of unresolved samskara's (habits) thereby brings crushingly forth much dissonance and dissension.

Consequently, our household was not incredibly harmonious in the lead up to the funeral and a prior booked trip to Bali. Everything was just a little off centre while they all tiptoed around my moods. Conor, my fiancé, was getting frustrated with me and my incapacity to handle the situation with ease or grace. He also worried whether the funeral would mean our trip to Bali would have to be cancelled or postponed. Before this, we'd been excited to be taking Conor's two daughters and my two children away. Juggling his kids could sometimes be tricky, because of past messy altercations with his ex-partner, mainly of my making. Conor and I had been in various stages of 'together' over the past five years.

He was mostly a good and generous man, the first attempt at a mature relationship I'd had. He was an adoptee of an Irish background with the classic traits of his nationhood. Generally of jovial mood, he liked a good 'drop', was always happy to 'chew the fat' over different real estate deals I had on the go. He often did the background research for me to follow through and contact the owners for interest in a sale for land development. We were mainly a 'good' partnership.

He was just over six feet, peaches and cream freckled complexion, caring and solemn brown eyes surrounded by the lines that show a person loves laughter. He also loved the more beautiful things in life and treated me like a 'princess', looking after me with dinners, holidays, loans and ridiculously expensive jewellery. His only downfall was the booze, probably not to the extent of my own demon battle though. I was fond of telling people at our engagement party that I fell in love with his three car wine cellar stocked with some of the best wines of the world before I fell in love with him. Somewhat indicative of where I was at that point.

In the lead up to the day and our impending trip, I was busy editing the three-hour conversation. I added in photos and some of Huey's favourite music so it could be used as a eulogy at his funeral and drinking bottomless glasses of wine at night to wind down. I was losing myself in work and alcohol, unable to face the ache within my heart of the loss of a loved one, the King of the Clan. Tensions within the household ran high. I was always quick to react, a fiery sun sign, Conor, a redhead. Fire meeting fire. Sometimes things became ablaze. To his credit, Conor mainly dealt with managing my kids, leaving me to my own devices. In a haze we made it to Perth for the funeral, luckily only having to delay our flight to Bali for a day, with minimal cost. I went up a day earlier to help my mum, and the rest of the family, Conor and the kids followed the next day. Conor seemed a little distant to me, but I didn't think much of it. I was caught up in the funeral undertakings, organisation and acknowledging my extended family. I sensed he was annoyed with me, but let it go. I didn't have the time or energy for it and imagined he was getting edgy as he usually did about travel that night. The ten-minute eulogy clip I had laboured over was received incredibly well with much kudos. I knew my grandfather would have been proud yet humbled to have been honoured in such a way. It certainly lit a lantern for future direction for me, in ways I could Serve. Emotionally though, I was still so raw, lacked sleep, and had simply pushed my feelings aside while I dealt with 'tasks.' It wasn't until I got to Bali that I could be in a space I could unravel them. If I had wanted to and Chose to.

We arrived in Bali in the early hours of the morning. By the time we reached the hotel, it was mid-morning and too early to get to our room. So, Conor and I did what we did together toxically well, sat in the Beautiful Balinese humidity in the hotel pool and began to drink various alcoholic beverages. The kids ran around playing, jumping in and out, ordering food, interacting as we 'unpacked' the events and moods of the last week. Not a good idea on little sleep, in the sun with alcohol. As these things inevitably did, the day ended in an argument though we both fell asleep reasonably early that night, with little comparative damage being done. Some of our past 'discussions' were like the beginning of World War Three.

Conor graciously kept the kids busy over the next four days or so taking them out so I could have some time to myself. He was probably also happy to stay out of my way. I slept a lot and read and sunned myself. I generally gave myself some time out. I went through the stages of grief and got caught in the anger. On the second last night, after a couple of pre-dinner drinks, we all headed out for dinner to a local restaurant we had frequented before. We enjoyed a meal together, laughing and joking, with Conor and I drinking some local cocktails and Bintang. We were blessed in our blended family got along pretty well. When we returned home, with the kids all settled in bed, we were having a nightcap of cognac, when I decided I'd like to go out.

"Are you okay with me going out?" I checked in. "I feel like dancing."

Conor knew better than to argue, though set his jaw. "Yep, if that's what you want to do," he responded.

I set about getting myself ready, fixing my hair, touching up my makeup. I kissed him goodbye and made my way out to the quiet Seminyak street, walking a little way before hailing a 'Bimo,' a local taxi.

"Apa Kapar," I said hello in Indonesian. "Can you please take me to the closest club?"

"Baik, Baik," said the driver, Wayan. "Yes, miss that will be Peanuts. It's the only one open now."

The club was a bit of a dodgy one, not one I would usually attend, not that I was attending clubs that often anyhow. I didn't care; I had pent up emotion that would be best danced off. It was pretty quiet, but the music was loud, and it wasn't long until they played something I could dance to. I strutted my way to the dance floor to the electronic beat, joining in the chorus, to Dizzy Rascal's 'Bonkers' song.

Playlist - Dizzee Rascal - Bonkers 2009

I gyrated my hips, waving my arms in the air, figure-eight undulating my shoulders and torso from side to side, swaying my way around the dance floor. I lost myself in the music for the next half an hour or so, eyes closed. Uninterested in dancing with anyone else, I wasn't seeking social interaction. I was invoking dance-therapy, merely allowing the music to define my next move, offering movement as the expression of my repressed emotions. I didn't care what I looked like. I wasn't trying to attract male attention, nor there to consume more alcohol. It was a cocktail creation of a motion-healing elixir.

Breathless, I decided to get some water from the bar. I was feeling euphoric and light-headed. As I was sipping some water from the bottle, I stepped back and felt something underneath my feet, too late, before a growl, and an incisor inserted itself in my right calf. In fear and shock, I made an involuntary shriek, and heard the Balinese around me saying, "Rab- I - ez, Rab -i - ez, Rab- i- ez."

RABIES!

A little white dog with a black studded collar was still growling at me and I limped my way outside to suss out the damage. In terms of pain, it was minimal, more of a fright than anything. There'd been a massive outbreak of Rabies on the island. I'd read about it since being there. They were talking about doing a mass cull of dogs; the infection was that rife. There'd been many cases of Rabies, with some fatalities. I sat on a chair and surveyed my leg. There were two piercing marks on my mid-right calf and two tiny drops of blood. It was not a scarring bite but possibly enough to carry the viral disease.

The reality of the situation began to sink in. I didn't know what to do.

But I thought if I stopped the blood from raising any higher in my leg, maybe I could stop the spread of Rabies to the rest of my body. This was misinformed. Don't try this at home. You're meant to wash the wound with soap and water. So I ripped off my top, luckily I was wearing a bra, and wrapped it around my leg creating a tourniquet. A young Balinese man came to assist me, asking me if I would like to be taken to the hospital. I gratefully agreed.

We must have looked quite a sight as we travelled to the International Medical Centre on his scooter, me on the back, topless except for a black bra, red and white gardenia skirt flowing in our wake. Though this was Bali and all degrees of standard dress could sometimes be lost amid mostly Australian party goers. They took me right through to the doctors as soon as the young man explained in Indonesian what had happened. There was no waiting, and expediently they washed my wound with soapy water, instructed me it was okay to put my top on, creating a tourniquet was not doing anything. (Oops!) They gave me the Rabies vaccination - post-exposure prophylaxis (PEP). A couple of million rupees later, I could leave. They armed me with an info sheet and instruction to visit my own doctor as soon as I landed back in Perth, thirty-six hours away, and to continue the treatment of four further Rabies injections.

I caught another Bimo back to the hotel where Conor and the kids were asleep, not really sure about what this bite meant in the big scheme of things at this point. At 2am, I woke him up and told him what happened. He was incredulous yet concerned. We discussed the day's plans, and I decided I would still go to the waterpark with him and the kids the next day as organised. I didn't want to interrupt the schedule as I'd already been mostly absent majority of the trip.

Some 'googling' before leaving the hotel had me beginning to realise the seriousness of the situation had the dog definitely been infected with Rabies. I quickly began to see the bite as a Gift, a wake up call, and an opportunity to make some changes, though I wasn't entirely convinced at this point. That would come later.

I didn't do a great deal at the waterpark. No thanks to headaches and nausea, I rested under the gazebo we'd hired. The next day we left for home after catching the plane from Bali to Perth. We then divided into our 'original' family blends to travel the three and a half hours in our separate cars back to Marg's. I saw my parents in Perth. Conor's girls needed to be back in Margaret River, so he left fairly imminently from landing After dinner, when my kids were in bed, and we'd unpacked, with lots of washing in the machine and the whirring noise of the dryer, Conor and I were sitting outside. While I smoked, we shared a bottle of local red wine.

"You know I've been researching Rabies, and it's quite unsettling," I said, head in my laptop.

"What?" questioned Conor, a little tetchily. "You should be right now you've had the first injection?"

"Well, apparently not," I began. "There was a case where a lady had all the injections, and then seven years later, she contracted Rabies and died."

"Well, why don't you get a test to see if you have it then," Conor offered as he swilled some wine. "You know I think this wine is getting better as it's getting older."

The merlot we were drinking was one he and some friends had made.

"Mmm... Yeah... you know, that's the thing," I said. "You can't be tested. It's undetectable until you actually have it, and once you have it, it's a death sentence. There's no way out of it but to die."

"Well, how do you know you have it?" asked Conor.

"Sometimes it's undetectable, you can become paralysed and slip into a coma, and people don't realise they've died from Rabies. Otherwise, you can literally start running around trying to bite people, getting all aggressive... You wouldn't wish it upon your worst enemy, it's pretty horrible."

"Not sounding so good," remarked Conor dryly. "So, we might have to tie you up like a dog," he laughed.

"Not funny," I retorted drinking some more wine, refilling our glasses from the almost empty merlot. "But the weirdest thing is that one symptom is you get an irrational fear of water. It's set off when you are offered some to drink, and it says here," I continued reading off a Health 24 site, "that other early signs are an inability to swallow, excessive saliva and aggressive, uncontrollable behaviour."

"But it's very rare, after the vaccinations, to develop Rabies, isn't it?" Conor clarified.

"Yeah, I think so," I answered, but it got me thinking. I wondered how I could or if you could even stop Rabies from developing if I fell in that very low almost impossible percentage of people who developed it after the vaccinations. So, I started to research that, typing, 'How to stop the development of Rabies' in the search bar.

I lit another cigarette, and absentmindedly said to Conor, "You know I saw Beth today, and she was quite weird."

Beth was a co-worker when I'd been employed in the corporate world, and she lived in the same neighbourhood. She was a slim, attractive curly-haired blonde, single mother of two. These days she was a confidant and a drinking buddy when I needed to run away from the domestic responsibilities of mothering four, having little space to myself. I would often stumble my way over to her house at about 9 or 10 o'clock when Conor was watching TV, and I wanted someone to talk and drink with.

"You know I have something to tell you about Beth," said Conor.

I was half-listening, caught in my reverie, paying more attention to the outcome of my research and Kings of Leon's 'Use Somebody', track from Only by The Night CD.

Playlist - Kings of Leon - Use Somebody 2008

The next words *I thought I heard.*

"You know that night before I headed up to Perth, before the funeral?"

I had gone up the night before everyone else to assist my family with my grandfather's funeral.

"Beth came over, and we had a couple of drinks, and stuff started to happen."

My ears perked up, and I became still.

"What?" "What the f**k did you just say?"

"Nothing."

"What did you just say about Beth? Repeat it," I demanded.

"Mandi, you are off your head. I said she dropped around, and we shared a drink. What did you think I said?"

"I - think - that - you - just - f**cking - said - that - you -slept - with - Beth - you -arsehole," I enunciated slowly, clearly and with teeming, building anger. He'd pushed a button, and I was seething red fiery flames. I had severe trust issues with Conor due to him being unfaithful, then sleeping with me unprotected before he told me about it, very early on in our relationship. So yeah, trust was an issue, particularly after drinking two-thirds a bottle of wine each. And then, astrologically speaking, my Chiron wounding was in Aries, thus insecurity and jealousy were always going to hit me right in the core where it counted.

"How- could – you? She's - my -f**king - friend. No - wonder - why - she - was - f**cking - weird - with – me."

I picked up my wine glass and threw the contents at him, blood red wine splattering his white shirt like a freshly severed tendon.

"F**king C**t."

I marched over to him and slapped him across the face with as much strength as I could muster.

Conor, infuriated, raised his hand and slapped me back.

I reeled away, turning on my heel, not wanting to take it any further.

"**Right. I'm going over there to sort this out. What a bitch.**" I violently pulled the sliding door open, slamming it shut, stomping and crashing my way through the house. Closing the front door, I stormed my way through the neighbourhood in ablaze of rage and anger.

It was 11pm. I bashed at Beth's' door. "**Beth let me in,**" I yelled as I hammered.

No response.

"**Conor told me what happened.**"

No noise from inside the house.

"**Let me in.**"

No reply.

"F**king tell me what happened."

No Response.

"Beth."

No response.

"Let me in."

No response.

"What the f**k."

No response.

"Beth why won't you even tell me what happened?"

No response.

I knew she was there. It was a Sunday night, school started the next day, and she was a night owl. She was always up at this time.

I was beyond reproach. I was so angry. I was f**king furious. How **could she**? I thought indignantly. They'd always flirted with one another. **I knew not to trust her.**

I was enraged. Past boiling point. And the alcohol I'd consumed was adding highly flammable propellant to my rabid fire.

I kicked one of the glass sidelights to the left of the door with my foot, and it smashed with the force. There was a sound of glass shattering.

Almost immediately, I regretted my actions.

My heart dropped into the pit of my stomach and settled there. I felt instant remorse for damaging the property, for scaring the shit out of her and her children, irrespective of what happened. And I began to doubt my own sanity.

"Oh F**k," I said. "I'm sorry, Beth, that was so f**king stupid."

I left and walked back to our house, full of remorse.

Embarrassed and ashamed, I also felt strangely empty. I poured myself another glass of wine and sat down in our front room away from Conor.

I didn't know what to think or what to believe.

Conor came in after a while and said, "Right, that's it, Mandi, it's over. I'm out of here tomorrow. No more. I've had it."

I didn't have the energy to respond, I just sat there. It felt like everything was finished.

A short time after, I noticed the flash of blue lights and the sound of a car pulling up in our driveway.

Within minutes, I heard a knock at the door.

Standing at the door were two police officers. I let them in.

"Good evening, I'm Constable Cooper, and this is my colleague Constable Reece," said the taller one with darker hair. "We are here there has been a neighbourhood complaint about a disturbance."

"Yes, I know. I know why you are here," I said, as I motioned them into the house. We settled on the couch.

"Can you please tell us what happened?"

I filled them in with the details, including why I'd done what I did. I was full of deep regret. I was incredibly humiliated by my actions. I was in disbelief. The rational side of my mind couldn't fathom how I'd managed to do what I'd just done.

The police questioned Conor, and he added in his side of the story.

The smaller one left saying he would drive around to tell Beth she was safe, that I was under control and remorseful.

His partner remained to talk with me. Conor left the room.

"Next time, no violence, hey?" he said.

"I know. I'm so sorry. I have had the shittiest fourteen days. My grandfather died. I got bitten by a dog that had Rabies in Bali. I just got back today. Then I find out my fiancé slept with an ex-work colleague while I was in Perth sorting out my grandfather's funeral. No excuses, I know. I just feel so incredibly mortified," I said through tears.

"Are you going to be okay?" Constable Cooper enquired, nodding his head in the direction Conor was in.

"Yes, he's leaving. Anyhow, it's over. I think it was over a long time ago," I reflected.

Constable Reece came back from Beth's house. "She's all okay. Doesn't want to press charges, is happy for you just to get it fixed as soon as possible, Mandi."

"Yep okay, I'll do that first thing," I said.

The police left then, and I was left with my own sincere regret and confusion.

Conor came in while I sat there and said, "I didn't sleep with her. What you said wasn't true." Then turned and walked out of the room, supposedly to sleep in one of his girls' beds. Thankfully, they were at their mother's house.

I don't recall the next part of the story. Apparently, after half an hour, while my kids slept, I started yelling his name out, trying to find him after I had searched the house to no avail. And ended up picking up a knife and looking for him with that in my hand, in the backyard calling for him. I don't have any memory of this. And therefore, don't know what I was doing with a knife in my hand, or what I might have done with it. Thankfully, we didn't find out.

He left after that. Without a word, he jumped over the side gate, quietly got in his car and stayed in a hotel fifty kilometres away after spending thirty minutes hovering in a bush fearing for his life.

And that was done.

Over.

The next day I woke up, feeling a lot sore and sorry for myself yet full of strange hope. I'd hit the bottom. The only place lower than where I was in my mind would be if I'd been picked up like a bag of scruffy bones from the gutter. I'd had enough. The strength of the last three events had rendered me and ushered me towards a turning point, a new door. Spirit had knocked, and initially, I didn't answer, but now I was tuning in. I was fine-tuning the dial. I resolved to make some massive changes to my life.

But first, the last hurrah.

I rang my friend, Anne, whom I knew had Mondays off and arranged to pick her up to come 'celebrate my break up' and 'my last drink for ten years.' I'm not sure she believed either. She'd heard the breakup line before, as had she listened to the 'last drink for a month', which I'd never stuck to. Ten years was a first. I arranged to pick her up at eleven-thirty that morning. In the meantime, I got my surly, tired, mistrusting and confused children, Kael and Aala, on to the bus and off to school. I'd promised them things were about to change for the better. Then I cleaned up the house a little.

I quickly showered, dressed in some 'going out' clothes, and applied some make-up. Next, I checked in with my appointment for the doctor and second Rabies injection the next day, organised the glass to be fixed on Beth's house, and headed out the door.

It was a beautiful spring day in October in Margaret River. The day was fresh and full of promise. It was a magical late morning to be driving with the roof off my black convertible, particularly through the magnificent Karri trees of Carters Road. Gorrilaz' 'Feel Good Inc.' pumped out of my stereo as I tuned in, the wind blowing the fresh air upon my face. Sparkly sunlight gently caressing and warming my skin. It felt good to be alive, a real turning point for me.

Playlist - Gorrilaz' - Feel Good Inc – 2005

My friend and I had a spectacularly indulgent and lavish extended lunch together at esteemed winery Leeuwin Estate. Champagne, oysters, crayfish; I was going out in style. Anne drove the car back into town. We picked our kids up from school and headed back to her house where we continued to drink a little more wine, and chat.

At about six, I made my way around the corner to another friend's house, Sam and Tim's. Sam prepared a delicious meal for us, and we shared some more wine. (This was 'wine country'.) After dinner, quite intoxicated by this point, I stumbled, slurring a little into a taxi with my two kids, to make our way home. We got ourselves to bed. Fully clothed, I fell into a heap upon the bed I'd shared with Conor, pulled the blankets up and passed out.

I woke up the next morning hungover but full of resolve. I had a shower, and got the kids up, made them and myself some breakfast. Today, October 19th, 2009, was Day One of my experiment of not drinking for ten years. #10yearexperiment. And the first day of celibacy for a year. These were my resolves Spirit had 'intuited', had 'dropped in for me' as a 'knowing' that had been confirmed with goosebumps. And this would be the guidance I would be 'tuned into' from now on. I would take my cues from above, as below base impulse wasn't working out so well for me.

I wanted to see what I could create.

I wanted to see what else was possible.

I wanted to be the Best version of myself.

I never wanted to see my kids looking at me with disgust in their eyes again.

I wanted to embark upon a path of purity.

I wanted to see what else was possible.

I got a taxi to drop the kids off to school, and help me pick my car up from Anne's, then ordered myself a coffee from the local. Gingerly, I greeted a few mothers of children I knew as I waited for my appointment to see the doctor for my next Rabies shot, working hard to keep my thoughts positive.

I was by no means ready for my world to be completely transformed in the way that it was about to be. In fact, if you tried to tell me, I would have laughed in your face! Today, Day One of my ten-year experiment, marked the beginning of the most magical unfolding of a decade that would render most people speechless.

Chapter Five

LEARNING TO LET GO

Aparigraha

Playlist – Beatles - Let It Be 1970

My two kids and I lived in Margaret River for almost a decade. In 2011, I had given up alcohol for eighteen months, and it was time for a change. Most of my friends had been 'drinking buddies' and after I stopped, so did the invites. It is too challenging for most to have a non-drinker in their midst, particularly in Margaret River, where most consume a bottle of wine a night as normality. I was a mirror most chose not to look in. We moved back up to our hometown of Perth as a unanimous decision to be closer to my mum as her health declined due to cancer.

My relationship with my mum, who was only eighteen years older than me, had always been fire-cracker-sharp, mellowing out to a fizzle once I'd had my children. Then we found some footing with which to build more positive affinity from, most of the time. Kael and Aala had a beautiful bond with their 'Nanna' though. She was everything wrapped up in what we want our grandparents to be, loving, caring, kind, thoughtful, with a genuine interest in their lives who languished time and gifts upon them. She made all her grandchildren believe that they were most special to her. As a result, they were happy enough to move their lives three hundred and fifty kilometres up the road, to start all over again. To spend some more quality time with their beloved Nanna before she passed beyond the veil.

At the roots of the discrepancy within my primary relationship with my mother lay abandonment and rejection issues. Sub-consciously, I felt abandoned by my mum for leaving me to be cared for by my dearly cherished grandmother while I was a baby to toddlerhood. Even though I was incredibly blessed to experience unconditional love from Ivy, my grandmother, it came at a cost. The price was a confused, agitated, often jealous and insecure, uncertain bond between my mum and I. Because of my grandmother spending more time with me, I naturally forged a stronger connection with her than with my mother. Thus, my grandmother's touch or arms would soothe, at my mother's resentful frustration.

At family get-togethers, if I was hurt or in pain, hungry or requiring comforting, it is my grandmother I would turn to because I had formed my primary relationship with her. This created an animosity for my mum as she innately felt I didn't like her, I didn't value her, that I was rejecting her. Which essentially is what I felt about her. That at the core, my mother had rejected me, and didn't value me. This cycle played out numerous times in our relationship with one another.

At age three when my sister, Melanie, was born, I struggled with what I perceived to be the attention I craved bestowed upon her. Again, I felt the 'lack of' love, abandonment and rejection all over again. My mum battled to accept the close affection between myself and her sister, Sue, as this bought up the same issues of rejection for her. In yogic terms, the most crucial lesson for healing with one another was a deeper understanding of the Fifth Yama of Patanjali's sutra Aparigraha. A capacity to let go of our past wounds and perceptions of how we had hurt one another and just show up for one another in the present moment.

"So, what does all of this mean? How many treatments are there?" I gently questioned Gina, my mum's doctor, as I sat in on my mum's check-up appointment at the hospital. There were four of us in the room, my mum, my dad, Gina - my mum's oncologist and me.

"It means there are five trial treatments we can access to treat your mum and that currently, we are on our second," she explained. "There are always more treatments being discovered, and your mum is doing incredibly well on this one."

"So, are we looking at a cure here or an extension of her life?" I swallowed as I asked.

"We are looking at extending her life with quality," Gina answered. "There is no cure for bone cancer."

My mum had battled with cancer for almost twelve years at this point. They'd diagnosed her at fifty with primary breast cancer which had already spread to her lymph nodes by the time they operated the first time. This lead to having the breast and some lymph nodes removed and a couple of bouts of chemotherapy and radiation. My rambunctious two-year-old son, Kael, was her only grandchild at that time, and he was the 'light' of her world, giving her greater reason to live. After celebrating the magic number five years clear, she was re-diagnosed about six months later. The cancer had metastasised into her bones as well.

"So you know I live in Margaret River, right? Well, what would you do in my shoes?" I asked.

"I'm not sure I understand your question," responded the oncologist in a clinical tone.

"Would you move up here, if you were me? Is it that time?" I implored.

"I cannot answer that question for you. We all choose how we prioritise our time. I don't know whether you choose to spend time with those you love."

And that was enough of a reason for me, so I was pleased when I put the suggestion to my children that they too, came to the same decision.

Before we left Margaret River, I caught up with a powerful clairvoyant who'd been a distant friend. She glanced over my shoulder, as she always 'saw' this way, saying, "You are going to honour and follow your sacred contract."

"Yes," I responded. "My mum is dying. There is healing to be done."

"Yes," she agreed, "but that is not all. You are meeting your soul family too."

In amongst the craziness of the move, I didn't give much thought to that comment. It only became relevant later.

***

We moved into a house north of Perth that Conor bought, five minutes away from my mum and dad's house, after 'semi-harmoniously' living with my parents for the first six weeks. Then I became busy with the move, re-establishing myself back in Perth, racing around after the kids with extra-curricular activities, new friends and fitting in **lots** of Hot yoga. Hot yoga was my saving grace. Our new house was exactly four minutes away from the studio by design. Including my own morning practice, most days, I practiced at least two and a half hours of yoga. The asana, moving meditation, was assisting me in maintaining equilibrium. To cope with the move and all of its demands. To help me deal with the fact I'd moved to Perth because my mother was dying and the finality of that reality. To offer me the reprieve and practice of non-attachment and non-grasping behaviour. On and off the mat I was practicing showing up 'in the moment,' with the breath. I'd let go of all that had come before and all that would happen, by just simply being with the inhalation and the exhalation.

One cold pyjama-clad morning after dropping my daughter off at the local school, a couple of cars up ahead, a car hit a little bluebird. I'm not sure if the vehicle that hit it even noticed. It didn't stop, and neither did I initially. Originally deterred from stopping because I was doing the school drop off in my pyjamas, my conscience got the better of me, so I retraced the route back to the bird. I ran out in my winter satin gold pj's and coffee-stained, white towelling dressing gown, complete with 'uggies' to check on the bird which was still actively trying to flutter its wings on the side of the road. As I got closer to it, I watched as it made its last move, took its last breath and died right before my eyes. I sent it blessings and thanked it for its contribution to the planet and for allowing me to witness its death. I scooped it up and gently placed it under some leaves on the earth, with some more prayers on the side of the road. I wiped a tear from my eye and walked back to the car, oblivious to oncoming traffic.

This experience happened about six months after our move into the new place and triggered some awareness for me. I realised although I'd moved to Perth to 'be with my mum,' I wasn't spending any time with her. I lived five minutes around the corner from her, as opposed to three and a half hours when I had been 'down south', yet we still weren't spending any time with one another. In fact, we probably used to spend more time when I was visiting on the weekends. We were putting no time into the relationship. My mum was busy with her own life, going away a lot.

I was feeling abandoned and rejected all over again. The 'core wound' was coming into play another time, whatever new skin that had grown over was getting picked away at, freshly dug at, allowing a little trickle of pus to leak out.

"Mum, I've realised although I live in such close proximity to you, literally around the corner, I'm not making any time for you, and it's making me feel really upset. I feel like when I was a child and I wanted you, but I had to stay with Nanny instead. I feel like I'm pulling and grasping at you, and you are nowhere to be found. I feel like everyone else gets to see you but me. I'm feeling rejected and abandoned at the same time," I explained as we shared a cup of tea the next day.

"Oh Mandi, I've been feeling a bit like that too. I thought you were too busy for me," Mum lamented as she pushed the scarf keeping her bald head warm back up her forehead.

So here we were, both experiencing the same thing from one another once more.

"Well I have been, I lost sight of my priorities for a bit, Mum, but I want to spend time with you. That's what I'm here to do," I said with tears forming in my eyes.

She reached to cuddle me, tears in her blue eyes too and I noticed how small and birdlike she felt. Frail, delicate, beautiful, fragile, child-like.

"Why don't we do a guided meditation together once a week?" she suggested.

We arranged a day, Friday, and began the following week. It was a practice we continued together every Friday until she passed. Together we explored the meditations supplied by Tiara Kumara's Children of the Sun activation series. Our capacity to speak about the situation and then make positive changes spoke volumes about the healing that had transpired between us. Before this, the natural 'outplay' of our relationship was slamming doors, yelling, emotionally shutting the other out, using emotional blackmail or any different 'wounded' behaviour pattern.

One Friday, we'd just listened to one of Tiara's guided meditations together, and I glanced across at the opposite couch at my thinning mother. Her mouth was wide open. Her skin looked grey. I panicked a little, and as I jumped up to check her, she opened her eyes and took a deep breath.

"Oh Mum, thank goodness. You scared me."

"Did you think I'd died?" She chuckled. "I must have fallen asleep."

Aparigraha in yogic terms refers to non-possessiveness, non-grasping, and non-greed. In the western world, it often depicts a movement towards non-materialism or only owning what we need. In my relationship with my mum, where we'd inherently struggled with feeling rejected by the other, we played out the concept of Aparigraha. We alternated in culminating frustration, with one of us grasping at the other in bitterness, and wanting to gain possession of the other, in a pendulum type effect.

This served as the inherent primary wound between us. We struggled between wanting to be with one another and turning our backs upon the other. This is what we set about to heal between one another, for one another, perhaps our sacred contract, the reason we were in each other's lives. And maybe even the reason I'd chosen her to be my mother. We also had to practice the ultimate of non-attachment - letting each other go.

My mettle was tested again just a couple of days before my mum passed. The second and only other time I had joined my mum at her appointment with the oncologist, I again asked the 'hard' question. "How much longer do you think she has?" And the overwhelming response - "A couple of weeks at most." We arranged to take my mum home with a script for enough morphine to dose up an entire football team. Her specialist had promised my mum when the end came, she would feel no pain.

One of the most poignant memories of that time was a conversation with my dad. He'd come into the hospital room after the appointment as he'd his own to attend. Can you believe checking on his lungs as suspected lung cancer? Thank goodness it was clear.

"Dad, it's not good," we quietly announced as he walked in the room.

'What, what do you mean?" he asked tentatively walking over to hold my mum.

My mum tried a wry smile as tears built up in her eyes, shaking her head at my dad.

"About two weeks, Dad."

"Ohhhhhhh Jan."

I saw my dad melt in front of my eyes. The look they shared is seared into my memory. It was all the love they'd shared in a lifetime of memories, knowing it was on a deadline now, had an impending finish line. And it would be time to let it all go.

My mum had many visitors over the last four days of her life, close family and friends. We had set up a 'hospice' style refurbishment of my mum and dad's bedroom, with my mum in a hospital bed, and my dad in a bed next to her. The Silver Chain came in daily to check on my mum, but primarily, we were responsible for her care.

The continual stream of visitors tested my practice of non-possessiveness and non-grasping all over again as I felt that core wound coming up. I just wanted to be with my mum. It's all I ever wanted. I didn't want to share her. I wanted her to myself. I felt my rejection and abandonment issues coming back up, and I struggled with it all again.

On the immediate day before she died, I'd been in my parents' house from seven in the morning till four that afternoon. In that time, I'd made numerous cups of teas for visitors saying their last farewells to my mum.

I'd gone out and bought more supplies, cakes, food for lunch and dinner, made small talk, smiled, did what was expected of me, and yet, hadn't spent **any** time with my mum.

I was struggling. I just wanted everyone else to go away. I was a child again, a baby. I just wanted my mum. Every single moment was now precious and suspended, yet the sand in the hourglass kept trickling down. When my former sister-in-law saw her for the second time, I couldn't contain myself any longer. I felt the emotion rise, the jealousy, the need I'd observed the whole day to be expressed. I implored my dad to help me, and thankfully he listened, and my daughter and I went in next.

Aala sat down on a chair adjacent to the bed. I crawled my way to my mum. I placed my head on her chest. Mum was tired, dozing, but she briefly opened her eyes. Part of me was disappointed she'd been awake and talking for everyone else and now she had no strength left.

"Mum, it's just been so hard. I just have wanted to be with you all day, but everyone else kept coming in."

She could not say so much at this point. She patted my head. I curled up into a ball, tears spilling from my eyes.

"Mum, I'm so sorry for everything I put you through. Did you get my letter?"

She nodded her head. "Mm-hmm."

I'd written her a letter five days ago upon hearing she didn't have much time to live. I apologised for my many wrong-doings, thanking her for my life, for all that she had offered, for allowing me to experience and fulfil my sacred contract.

"I forgive you, Mandi, it's okay," she said in between laboured breaths.

I pushed my head into my mum like a three-year-old would do. Afterward this is what my daughter said I looked like. She'd never seen me in such a vulnerable state before. The tears leaked out of my eyes as I buried myself back into my mother.

Oh, how I wish.

Playlist – Adele - Someone Like You 2011

My daughter sang the Adele song in her sweet pre-teen love immersed voice. It was a painful, poignant and excruciatingly, beautiful moment. And then we had to let go.

Chapter Six

PATH OF PURIFICATION

Saucha

Playlist - Deva Premal and Miten - Om Asatoma 2002

As my understanding of the 'don'ts' of my behaviour grew through different life experiences, a pathway to the 'do's' emerged with greater clarity as is re-iterated in Patanjali's second limb of yoga - the 'Niyamas.' Strangely as humans, it is always easier for us to decide what it is we don't want, to define what it is we do. The first of these niyamas, Saucha or purity, is the one I began to 'quest in' earnestly when I made my resolve to remove alcohol from my life for ten years and almost simultaneously commit to a daily practice, as well as celibacy. These formed the first building blocks that allowed me through 'tapas' - will power - to commit to myself, involution and evolution, rather than self-destruction. I have heard the highest of all light is only attracted to 'play' with a similar frequency. So, if we want to work in the uppermost echelons in a spiritual sense, we must

be that purity. I listened to the guidance of my awakening spiritual heart for the first most significant instructions, and then heard in time as further direction unfolded.

As per treatment requirements after a suspected Rabies bite, in 2009 on the day after my Leeuwin Last Harrah, Day one, I had a scheduled appointment for my first post-exposure prophylaxis (PEP) vaccination in my hometown of Margaret River. I'd contacted the doctor's surgery directly upon arrival to make sure they had the PEP, and to ensure the way it was handled through transportation was with great care. It was an incredibly expensive medication - about three thousand dollars for four treatments, and if not kept cold, the effectiveness of the treatment was significantly reduced. As I was injected with the drug, the doctor, a person I knew socially ran through the possible side effects.

"Okay Mandi, so it's possible you might experience headache, nausea, abdominal pain, muscle aches, and dizziness through this medication. Also, some low-grade pain to the site of injection and if you develop anything more severe, get back in touch as soon as possible," informed Dr Lou.

I received the shot in the deltoid muscle of my arm and thanked the doctor, then walked a little around town, looking for trinkets for my altar. Part of my plan in this 'clean-up' was to add a daily yoga sadhana (practice) into my life too. There was an alcove in the house that would make a perfect altar space, and as I planned to start practicing the next day, I wanted to set it up with some things today. I found a beautiful white buddha, which would be the cornerstone of my altar. It would be like praying first thing every day as I offered my practice to it. I decided to provide it with flowers and crystals, some fresh fruit and lollies too. After an hour, I made my way back to my car, purchases and groceries for dinner ensconced in my arms, excited to set it all up at home.

Things didn't quite go to plan. I managed to set my altar up and then had to lie down as I started to develop a fever. I sweated and fevered with the 'dog medicine' for the next four days, and I lost eight kilograms in weight over that space of time. I had vivid nightmarish visions and dreams. The PEP injection assisted me in purging through sweat a lot that no longer served me. I have no doubt this also included the internal toxins, both internally and entities externally that may have come by way of alcohol. By the weekend, I was weak but feeling much clearer. Having endured the worst of it, I felt like I was now able to commit to a daily asana and meditation (dhyana) practice and this began in earnest as of October 26th, 2009.

With committed practice, awakening at 5am every day, to devote at least an hour and often times one and a half hours to my practice on the ground in front of my altar, a space I kept debris-free, my body and mind began to regain strength and increased clarity. I devoted time to praying to myself really. Though I had a physical altar with a Buddha and other monuments of value, what I was really doing was dedicating time and space to **myself**. I was respecting and honouring myself, creating a beautiful sacred place externally and internally to 'house' spirit. Day after day, before breath, asana, and meditation, I drank a couple of drops of Doterra Lemon oil in warm water to get my sluggish digestive system working first up. I began to care much more for my physical body I'd trashed through over-indulgence in many other different ways as well. The Path of Purification paved out its own process unravelling one step to me at a time. One decision led into the next, somewhat like following breadcrumbs to who knows where. I had little knowledge or insight to understand the importance of the impetus or the trajectory I was on. I had to go to sleep earlier at night as I was tired due to getting up so early every day to practice, which re-established healthier sleeping patterns for the physical body. My body began to crave healthier food options, and I took more notice of what I was feeding and watering my Temple with. What 'flowers' did I consecrate, dress, and decorate my Temple with?

After being the renowned self-titled 'queen of quick' cook for many years, fast and processed foods began to disappear from our diet, and I added in more fruits and whole foods, though I still looked for options that had less preparation time. I stopped using pain killers, placing less stress upon my liver and kidneys. I didn't have any hangovers, so they really weren't necessary anyway. I saw an alternative practitioner that offered acupuncture and Chinese medicine to support detoxification of the organs my lack of previous care had placed under stress. I started each day with the mental attitude of Gratitude, taking time to offer thanks for that which I was receiving. Always first and fore-mostly was recognition of my Breath, the Inhalation, and the Exhalation. The fact I was still alive and granted this experience of Life. The idea of putting Botox in my body, which I explored twice, now seemed a ridiculous idea. Why would I want to poison my body with that?

Although I wasn't sure what I did want at this point, aside from being the best version of me possible, it became clear on what I didn't want. There were lots of 'not doing this, not doing that,' that were given to me intuitively, dropping in one after another, in the process of being the 'purist', 'cleanest' possibility of me.

"Not drinking alcohol."

"Not eating sugar."

"Not having processed foods."

"Not staying up all night."

"Not being around people drinking."

"Not going to the pub."

"Not going out."

"Not eating fast food."

"Not having sex."

As time went on, more balance came in as 'I am doing this, I am doing that.' Basically, I paved the way for my 'inspiration' or 'spirit' to communicate better with me. I picked up a couple of yoga classes a week both at the local gym and with a couple of instructors. I became more interested in the yogic path, committing to 'purifying my mind' also and read voraciously in the field. I had not watched the news nor read a state media publication for the past five years. Now I firmed that resolve, wanting to keep my mind 'clean'. I also became aware of the language I used, cleaning up my conscious mind.

A couple of my 'classic' go-to statements had to be rehashed and revamped.

"No worries."

"Not a problem."

"I can't wait."

These statements created a negative outcome, although they were intended to express positive intent. So out they went in my sweeper path of purification and in-coming was:

"All good."

"Great."

"Awesome."

"I'm so looking forward to…"

I made a conscious effort to eliminate swearing, really purifying my communication and conversation, as well as cleaned up my music and movie selections. What mantras was I feeding myself, what vibration did different things carry? What was I watching, reading? How did it make me feel? What and who lowered or raised my vibration? It all became a constant field of inquiry as I focussed on this path of purification on every level I could possibly fathom. I stopped dyeing my hair, allowing it to grow out from the high maintenance 'Uma Thurman - pulp fiction bob' into a more natural look. I became a continuous work in progress, the beacon of discernment, shining the torch over every area of my life. Nothing was left immune. Rather than lamenting, or getting caught up in guilt over past action, I allowed and offered myself the freedom to grow in fresh new directions as guided by the Light. Through my inner subjective work, the involution, everything externally began to grow and evolve. This meant benefits all-around in my relationship to self, and my children, my lucidity and my connection to my intuition or 'higher self.' That little tinkle of ancient stardust, that cosmic voice that had been trying to grab my attention now had free reign. I had crowned it and now allowed it to be heard and acted upon. I listened to that voice through my awakening Spiritual Heart. My ever-expanding path of purification led to higher self-worth, and more 'self' power, through the unadulterated empowerment of the self in its purest most authentic, unpolluted version and I began to shine ever so sparkly and bright.

Outwards my scope extended. I looked at cleaning products I was using, looking at the detrimental effects of popular products, becoming alert to genetically modified foods, boycotted goods that used palm oils or harsh chemicals, finally gave up smoking cigarettes. My practice deepened, and anything detrimental or unhealthy for my body just fell away. I stopped eating red meat, then white meat, dairy, then seafood. Ceased drinking coffee and took up copious amounts of herbal tea instead and spring-fed fresh non-fluoride water, such as Apostle. Interestingly, due to the freedom from the matrix of alcohol and non-drinking state, I craved sugar. I was so used to a large weekly consumption of sugar in the wine I drank, that when I stopped, I discovered a screaming sweet tooth demanding to be fed, enough to make me wonder if I might have been nourishing an ulterior motive all along. Was the sugar I consumed as a by-product in the alcohol I drank responsible for the mood changes that occurred? An interesting ponder. To keep the sweet tooth happy, I began to experiment with making and purchasing 'healthy chocolate,' cacao and coconut oil, with honey or agave and a couple of drops of Doterra orange or peppermint oil. Allowing myself one or two pieces a night. Finding moderation and satiation in that.

The removal of alcohol instigated the most massive clean-up for me. I said to a close friend in conversation once, "I gave myself twenty-five years of drinking and debauchery, (from age fifteen to forty.) If I couldn't offer a decade to experiment with the state of alcohol-free then surely this would indicate I had a 'problem' with alcohol." (#10yearexperiment)

An interesting statement in itself and not one many of us give much thought to when growing up in a western society such as Australia. We are notorious drinkers, much to many other cultures' distaste. I know for me, once I stopped drinking, the thought of hanging out in Bali with all of the 'drinkers' over there 'just having fun' letting their hair down was not one I resonated with, nor actively sought out. In fact, I purposefully refrained from going to places where there would be alcohol for almost seven and a half years because I didn't want my energy field infiltrated with the 'entities' known to attach themselves to people who drink copious amounts of alcohol and use drugs. I had done a lot of work to purify my own energy field, I didn't want others to infiltrate my purity.

Alcohol is such an ingrained part of the Australian culture. Related to most things we do socially, it has been such an interesting journey to renounce this. Many of us experiment with contraband liquor from our parents in early adolescence and never even contemplate the possibility we can put it down. My alcohol-free stance has been the topic of many conversations along the same lines. So many people have said to me, "Oh, I don't drink either."

"Oh, really," I would contend. "So, when was the last time you had a drink?"

"Oh, well, I had a glass last weekend. I only ever really have a glass every now and again."

"Ah, so it's not really **not** drinking then is it?"

Most people don't understand the effect alcohol has upon their subtle bodies and will justify their drinking with much voracity. Not realising this whole use of alcohol, in my perspective, keeps them rooted in societal programming, the matrix, ensuring they remain slaves to the system. Science shows us even one drink affects the mood, the subtle energy bodies, and the physical body. For me, my most considerable growth has come by choosing not to consume alcohol. There has been way less drama. Let's face it, I'm a Leo - sun and moon. There's probably going to be a little drama from time to time, it comes with the territory. However, since my ten year experiment, things don't get out of control and nor do they exacerbate. Since I stopped the consumption of alcohol and dedicated myself to a daily practice, I have dealt with the death of my mother, the end to a long term relationship, moving numerous times and many other stressful triggers that previously might have taken the wheels off my roller-skates and sent my life careening who knows where. Though the wheels have remained on, and decidedly so.

Choosing celibacy also contributed to keeping my energy field clear and was a continuation of my path of purity. That first year of my ten-year resolve, following the path of purification, I allowed myself a year's opportunity to follow the more austere, single blessedness path of a yogi, and then again for a subsequent four years from years five to nine of my ten-year experimentation. Combined with the break from alcohol incredulously created the path of a 'Great Sacrifice' in Western terms, likened to the closest one might get to an Indian Sadhu's renunciation or a dramatic display of Austerity. In India, where yoga derives from, an act of 'great sacrifice' might be to raise an arm for ten years without allowing it to fall manifesting as a withered expression of the arm due to a lack of blood flow, or maybe to fast for copious lengths of time, or to be silent for a number of years. Here, in Australia, I have found people most impressed and see me as an inspiration due to my choices - great sacrifices - through the renunciation of drugs, sex, and alcohol. Oh, what a fascinating, wonderfully weird world we live in. That it could be such a 'thing' to sacrifice 'drinking,' to go against the grain of societal way of life. That one could become an inspiration by purely non-engagement of sexual relations or alcohol. Plainly that speaks volumes of our society and how out of balance it has become.

From here we swing and sway to the next branch on Patanjalis' 'tree of life'. That of contentment.

Chapter Seven

SATISFACTION

Santosha

Playlist - Rolling Stones - (I Can't Get No) Satisfaction 1965

Satisfaction is not something Western Society wants us to find. If we are satisfied with where we are, what we are doing, what we have, who we are, who we are with, the way we look, and what we want. In effect, IF we are content with our lives, then we are no longer **consumers**. And consuming keeps the money going round, the money going round, the money going round.

In the ancient yogic myths, Patanjali's sutra's speaks of 'Santosha' or contentment. It is not something many of us who herald from a Western world experience throughout this lifetime. We always want more. Wanting what our neighbour has, wanting to lose weight, to gain weight, to buy a new dress, to upgrade the car, the phone, the house, your job, your partner. Or a computer, washing machine or any other commodity we find in a modern-day home or lifestyle. On the path of a yogi or yogini, we learn to be accepting of what we do have and let go of our attachment to gaining what we don't have. We discover and get to practice on the mat learning to be comfortable with where we are. As our practice deepens, we learn to let go of the need to master a specific yoga pose, to push ourselves beyond our limits. We learn to let go of the desire to buy a new mat, unless we actually need to, or the latest yoga pant craze. Or whatever other fan-dangle invention put into the marketplace of a now billion-dollar industry. Yoga is now apparently the highest growth industry in the world. We learn to just be happy with what we have, and where we are in the present moment because it simply is. In that 'is-ness' we find contentment and satisfaction, not fleeting, but everlasting, refreshing breath by breath, inhalation and exhalation.

When I was twenty-four, my best friend, Stacey, died. I was living at home with my parents. I still vividly recall that Wednesday morning I got the news. My dad had bought black and gold brand cornflakes that tasted more cardboard-like than the cheap box they came in. I was complaining about his poor choice of selection when the landline rang. Mum answered and passed the phone to me. It was Stacey.

"Mans, they found something in that cat scan, I just got the call," she told me, straight to the point.

"What? Oh My God! What did they find?" I said, trying to remain calm.

'I have a huge brain tumour. It's covering most of my brain."

"Oh no Stacey, I am so sorry to hear that," I said, trying my best to keep up. I gulped. "What are they going to do?"

"They say there is not much point in operating. There's only a small chance I will come through, but I'm willing to give it a go," she said softly.

"What?" I gulped. Stacey and I had been close for five years. Despite an age difference of eight years, we had been fast and furious friends from the moment we met in the northern cape of Western Australia. And I had become an 'un-official' godmother to her two kids, Caleb and Freya. She had just turned thirty-two. "When?"

"I have to go to Sir Charles Gardiner hospital this afternoon. They will operate on Friday," Stacey explained.

That was two days from now.

"Oh Stacey," I lamented. "Are you okay? Do you need me to do anything?" I was struggling to find the words, to remain on top of the quicksand of emotion threatening to drag me under with each further moment as the reality became more apparent.

"It will be all right. Mum's coming to look after the kids," she said. "I just wanted to call and let you know."

"Oh my God! Thank you... not thank you... oh, you know what I mean. I appreciate you letting me know. I'll come up and see you," I stuttered and promised.

I got off the phone in shock and spent the rest of the day dumbstruck. I knew something was wrong with Stacey. I'd seen her have epileptic style fits. I'd commented on her recent difficulty with communication, heard her complaints about headaches over the last six months. I fully supported, even actively encouraged her demanding a scan from the doctors. To explore deeper and further, to get to the bottom of what was going on with her health. She'd been to the doctors several times over the past couple of months. They'd just offered more hardcore pain killers. In my naivety, never did I imagine a brain tumour to be an outcome.

I visited Stacey the next day at the hospital, while her mum and other family members were up there. I tried to remain positive. To keep the visit light and upbeat. It was difficult to speak from the heart as there was no space for us to do so. It was a forced conversation.

She was typical Stacey. She'd had someone sneak in some contraband 'Gin and Tonic UDL's' and was going outside to smoke cigarettes. I consciously knew our time for one another was possibly almost over. Simultaneously, I utterly could not fathom when I left that there may be a reality I would never see my dear friend again. We said goodbye, surrounded by her other loved ones, but it didn't feel like 'the goodbye' you say to someone before you absolutely never see them again. I drove off from the hospital in a blur of jumbled and confusing heightened emotions.

Early that evening I picked up my 'Fly In, Fly Out' boyfriend, Troy, from the airport, and had a crazy night with him as we usually did. His first night back we drank a lot of alcohol and popped an 'acid trip'. We sat at the Ocean Beach Hotel, just across the road from infamous Cottesloe Beach, drinking beer and Bundaberg rum. I lamented my inability to cope with the fact I may never see my friend again. My long, curly-haired, crazy boyfriend suggested we go into the hospital and see her. It was eleven at night. Although a small part of me recognised it was probably not a good idea, the majority voted to do it.

Troy drove my 'yellow roller-skate' vehicle into the public hospital in Nedlands. By this stage, we were pretty much 'off our faces.' The LSD trip had kicked in and though we were past the 'liquorice all sort,' psychedelic stage we were still far from any 'normal' perception of reality. We'd taken a hallucinogenic after all.

After 'scouting' the hospital like some sort of action-adventure heroes, we discovered visiting hours were over (no shit, Sherlock) and we would have to 'commando in.' Which is what we did. Troy suggested I get into a wheelchair while he squatted down and hid behind me. He catapulted out 'James Bond' style when we reached the lift, doors opening and closing before the security guard had time to stop us. We went straight up to Stacey's floor and made our way to her private room. She opened the door before I knocked.

"Mans, I knew you were coming."

Our relationship had always been intuitive, knowing when the other was phoning or needed the other.

"They gave me drugs to put me to sleep, but I couldn't sleep. I knew you were coming. I knew this afternoon wasn't the last time I would see you," Stacey said. "Look at me Mans."

Stacey was standing in a hospital gown, her head smoothly shaven, a beautiful golden egg, no hair left. She was glowing and looked the best I'd seen in quite some time.

"You look gorgeous Stace," I gushed. "You're all radiant and glowing. You look amazing."

The gravity of the situation reduced the effects of the alcohol and the acid. We spent a poignant twenty minutes together, speaking to one another from the depths of our heart. Stacey asked me to look after her kids if she didn't come through - to keep an eye on them. We told each other how much we loved one another; how much we'd valued our relationship. We said we would see each other again, even if it wasn't on this earthly plane. She thanked me for coming up, she really appreciated it. It seemed she'd reached a level of santosha, contentment and acceptance of where she was at.

She was showing me how to be open to the natural flow of life. Within that teaching, she was also teaching me how to surrender to something greater than herself and practice Ishvara pranidhana. To be open to life's ever-unfolding emergence, with the utmost of Ease and Grace. Though like many other lessons, I was Gifted through witnessing or proximity to those experiencing, I was to gain practical knowledge in this for myself and was not content with learning through another.

When we left, I knew I wouldn't see her again. I was feeling depressed as we drove off. The rush of visiting her gave way leaving in its wake a despairing hopefulness. They'd given her a twenty percent chance of surviving the operation. And despite my feeling otherwise, part of me wanted to hang on to that faithfully. Troy and I went back to stay in the room we'd booked at the Ocean Beach Hotel. We awoke, checked out at ten o'clock in the morning, and went back to his house.

I received the news just after lunchtime. My dear friend hadn't made it through. My last vivid memory is of her was in the hospital gown, big smile, luminous and shining. "Look at me, Mans."

I didn't deal with her death well. I went through fury, smashing full bottles of red wine against a white wall. It was quite a spectacular artistic creation. I drank alcohol and smoked copious amounts of cigarettes. I grieved her loss, for my loss and for her children's loss who were still very young and would never know their mum. I tried to just 'hang out' with Troy on his week of 'typical' R and R but there wasn't much that fit into the 'normal' category about me.

Her funeral was a sad and solemn affair, and there was barely a dry eye. I was not really much in my 'head'. I think I was in a state of shock. They diagnosed her on a Wednesday and less than two days later, she'd died. There wasn't much time to come to terms with things, to navigate the situation in an emotionally mature manner, even if I'd the skills to do so. Which I'm not sure at that point I had.

Before the funeral, I noticed a horrible smell emanating from my lower region when I went to the toilet. After a doctor's appointment, it turned out I'd left a tampon in for about seven days. That's how unconscious I was to even my own bodily functions. My coping mechanisms were failing.

Troy's week off ended, and he headed back up to work despite being concerned about how I would fend for myself upon his departure. He offered to stay with me, but I refused. Troy ended up compromising, making me promise to see my doctor and get on some antidepressants to help me through this period. He left me with a friend to care for me, an old drinking buddy who was also a drug counsellor, Margie.

She had all the right qualifications, but we were not good for one another.

At the point of his departure back up to the mine site, I was in a state where I was feeling my own state of completion and contentment. I felt I'd experienced enough of this life and was happy to leave the planet. I'd dealt with much suffering and pain through my life up, and equally experienced so much joy and bliss. I felt comfortable that if it were my time to go, I would welcome it.

These frank conversations, like to whom I'd gift my possessions, had Troy anxious for my welfare. It made him uneasy about leaving me to go back to work in the mine site for the next six weeks. I dropped him at the airport and made my way to my doctor's appointment.

"My best friend died a couple of weeks ago, and my boyfriend suggested I come here and get antidepressants," I declared.

"How are you feeling?" the doctor enquired.

"I feel like I've had enough. Like I want to pack up my toys and go home. I've had a good life. It's had a lot of suffering, and a lot of good stuff too."

"Okay, I'll write you a script for Zoloft. If you make it through the weekend you should be okay," she said matter-of-factly.

I got the script filled and had lunch with some friends of Troy's. It was a date he'd set up so they could phone him afterward and he could receive a report on how I was. Then I made my way back to South Fremantle from north of the river to stay with Margie. Through this whole period, I was 'meant' to be living with my parents, although they were the last people I wanted to be around.

***

Playlist - Lenny Kravitz - Fly Away 1998

I wandered around with Margie over the next couple of days in an alcoholic haze. I was celebrating, my life, Stacey's life, Margie's life, life itself, and in 'preparation' mode. I'd never been a full-on drinker. Sure I 'binge drank' regularly on a weekend night and sometimes this extended over the whole weekend, Friday, Saturday and Sunday night. Rarely had I been the drinker who started at lunchtime or even before.

"Let's get some Champagne," I suggested at ten in the morning, the second day of my stay. "It's lunchtime in Sydney, and I need to get more cigarettes anyway," I justified. I was carrying around three different brands, depending upon which style the moment suited. Benson and Hedges - my main staple, soft pack of Kent and Peter Stuyvesant.

"Yep, great, I need some more too," said Margie.

She wasn't working at the moment as she was on stress leave. I wasn't working because I had taken leave without pay when Stacey died. So we were partying. And it was a Sunday. We must have made three or four trips up to the bottle shop that day, buying one more bottle of cheap champagne each time. Driving in Margie's beautiful, old sea green Chrysler valiant for the first couple, then walking up for the rest. Must have kept the attendants pretty amused. Then after four bottles, Margie decided we should go out to Cottesloe to her friends' place, another counsellor, Peter, to be close for the Sunday Session there which was pretty epic. We drove, somehow making it safely without injuring anyone on the road or ourselves, nor getting pulled over for drink driving.

We drank some more at Peter's; I was having fun, letting go of my melancholy, and letting my hair down, dancing, laughing. Before long the three of us went to the Cottesloe Hotel where we continued to drink some more. I was in a particularly raucous state and created quite a spectacle, dancing on tables, stumbling, until we, mainly Margie and I, were asked to leave at about seven o'clock. We decided to order some pizza and to stay in Peter's loft-style flat just across the road from the beach for the night. The food brought me down a little, making me a little sleepy, though I was still edgy. Peter offered me a massage to help me relax. We go into his bedroom where he massages my neck, and my back, long strokes. I am lying on my front, with very little on but a G-string. I feel his hands moving a little on my breasts, and before I know what is happening, I feel his penis thrusting into me. I clench up and tell him to stop, but he pays no attention and continues. I am too inebriated to do anything about it except bury my head into the navy satin sheet. He is strangely loving and kind afterward as if it is something I wanted.

I feel pretty devastated. I am in love with Troy and have been for numerous years. Despite hooking up together a couple of times over the past couple of years, this is the first time we have officially been together. There is nothing I wouldn't do to sustain this relationship. I would not sleep with another guy as there is no way I would risk threatening my relationship with Troy. This is not what I wanted to happen. I get up from the bed saying I would sleep on the couch. Making my way into the kitchen, I noticed an array of tablets, sleeping tablets, major and minor tranquillisers, painkillers. I take an assortment of ninety-six individual tablets and make my way back to the couch and lay down to die.

And I did die that night.

***

I rebirthed from the blackness fast and furious, biting a thermometer in half and swallowing the mercury end. The staff at Sir Charlie Gardiner public hospital worried I would then die from mercury poisoning. They'd already bought me back once after the ambulance arrived at Peter's house in Cottesloe. They'd pumped my stomach, given me charcoal, and recalibrated my heart.

I was seething.

I'd made my choice and I no longer wanted to live. I was happy with my experiences. I no longer chose to be on the planet.

It was my choice, surely.

Margie had found me not long after and called the ambulance. I stayed in the psych ward of the hospital for two weeks, a legality after a suicide attempt. It was a hilarious stay. My fury lessened with the alchemy of laughter. I met people who'd tried to end their life by flushing themselves down the toilet. How they thought they would make it through the S bend was a source of riotous rolling around on the ground style laughter. Another by driving a car off a cliff. Yet another by trying to hang themselves. We just laughed our way through. Laughter was our medicine. We would sit outside with our cigarettes and coffees, telling hysterically absurd stories to each other. Some of them weren't actually that humorous, but we all found them side-splitting anyway.

I wasn't prescribed any drugs. The doctors didn't see me as depressed; they saw my 'attempt' as situational. Troy flew down immediately and was injected with Valium. He didn't cope very well with the news. I decided to take a break from alcohol. My actions devastated my parents and family, and I think I made many people feel quite uncomfortable.

While there, a human-angel named Adam visited me. I didn't know him well. We'd been party acquaintances until that point, bumping into each other randomly from time to time over a few years. Or perhaps synchronistical in hindsight. After hearing the news, Adam felt compelled to see me in the hospital. Wallpapering my room with dolphin posters, he bought me dolphin oracle cards, a dolphin sarong, and placed a half-metre tall, basketball diameter, quartz crystal in my room. He set a **clear** intention for healing. Adam also suggested I come to the coastal town where he managed a bar, and he and his girlfriend lived. He encouraged me to get out of the city for a bit, to get away, offering me the opportunity to work with the two of them. It was a spectacularly good proposal for me as Troy was due to fly out on an extended trip in a matter of months, and my old life didn't seem to fit anymore.

I started to come to terms with the fact that I'd been unsuccessful in ending my journey despite giving it a **really** good shot. I concluded that perhaps I was actually meant to be here on the planet. Right or wrong, I believed maybe I'd some Work to do here. That I was here for a Reason, a Purpose. And also, perhaps misguidedly, a deep sense of knowing that I was Invincible, Unbreakable, and Undying.

A couple of weeks later, I left for the coastal town, as invited by Adam, to work in a restaurant as a waitress, with little more than a backpack. My healing began, orchestrated through the magic of Mother Nature. I witnessed and absorbed the most majestic of all sunsets. And the pindan, iron-rich red earth, the turquoise blue of the ocean, vibrant reds, royal purples, cerulean and black ink skies, populated with infinite, shiny bright stars. As each sensational thirty-degree day unfolded, lying in the golden rays of the sun, swimming with dolphins in a warm, inviting and cleansing sea fulfilled me. I re-emerged into a version of my 'self' that had not until this point fully been explored.

Deep in my genetic coding, unlocked through the magnificence of being in the Great Australian Outdoors, I realised I was greater than the suffering and the illusion I'd suffocated myself with. The wild and untamed beauty of the West Australian Northern aspect held me in my vulnerable state of fragility. I supported the external offering from Gaia through eating a healthy diet with lots of fruit and vegetables. I connected with the Sacred and Essential truth of 'me' through walking daily for an hour along the beach to my final destination of a robust 'energy' portal. Here I danced, nude, free and with abandon, and practicing some yoga asana and meditation. They housed me in a tiny two-by-two metre room with a single bed, a desk and a wardrobe. I spent most of my time outdoors, connecting back in with Mother Earth and her natural therapeutic forces. And for some time with very little but the elements, nature, the love of good people, and enough money to survive upon, I lived in this heavenly space of Santosha and Contentment.

Chapter Eight

THE PATH OF AN EXPLORER

Tapas

'I will to will thy will.'

Playlist – Melanie - Ruby Tuesday 1975

I was born two weeks early and with forceps, pulled from my mother's birthing canal by my right foot. The rest of my body was to follow. I lay flat, stretched out, gratefully embracing the space I'd lacked over the last couple of weeks. My mum was 4'11 1/2 and tiny. I was not a sweet, snuggly baby who wanted to re-live the womb environment for emotional security. Instead, I was incredibly joyous to be inhabiting my own 'area,' to be in my human body, and keen to explore my new habitat.

It is said I was born with a lot of determination and will power. In numerology I was a '1' and a Leo, thus destined to be comfortable with my independence. I met all the developmental milestones early. Walking at just under nine months old, I was on the move and wanted to speed through this initial dependent stage as quickly as I could. I had a natural inclination towards exploration and inquisitiveness. This meant they leashed me and led me around like a not so obedient dog, otherwise, I took off on adventures.

Climbing stairs, meeting people, I always wanted to know what was beyond the barriers my parents contained me within. And I paid no attention to what my mother tried to tell me as I didn't recognise her as my authority figure. That was my grandmother. I had my own mind and will.

In yogic terms, 'Tapas' the third branch of Patanjali's niyamas, refers to austerity and discipline, and building the internal fire. Being a fire sign, I'd an abundance of raging inner fire. My parents agreed with a request to try gymnastics at eight, and it was love at first try for me. I enjoyed learning of my body's capabilities, to gauge its dexterity, discovering what I could achieve with dedicated practice and training. I attempted new and more difficult expressions as my skill level expanded. My favourite apparatus was the floor and the beam. I loved the creativity, dance and freedom of expression these allowed, more than the stringent acrobatic prowess the bars and vault required.

My love affair with gymnastics lasted until I was just over fifteen, culminating with working towards achieving level nine and becoming a member of the Elite Squad for our club. My highest aspiration was to go to the Olympics and be just like Olga Korbut or Nadia Comaneci, and I trained hard, working towards this childhood dream.

Gymnastics was both a sport and an art. It required diligence, learning to control the body as an instrument of high precision and offered the opportunity to investigate and experiment within the human form. A course in physical and mental mastery, effectively learning how to drive my new 'vehicle' through the most arduous of terrains with Ease and Grace. Single-pointed focus Sanskrit and Patanjali refers to this as 'Dharana.'

I learned the value of a balanced, nutritional diet. It steered my consumption into healthy alternatives. And I learned which fuel my body required to perform optimally at a very young age. Furthermore, it encouraged my capacity to think and decide for myself. Gymnastics coated me in the discipline.

"Mandi, come and have some lunch, it's twelve o'clock," my mum yelled out.

"I'm not hungry," I declared.

"It doesn't matter. You must eat otherwise you won't have energy," she implored.

"Yes, but only if I'm hungry. The wise old men of Zen ate when they were hungry, slept when they were tired, and drank when they were thirsty," I told my mum.

"Last time I looked; you weren't an old man of Zen," my mum quipped.

I must have driven her mad.

Various aspects of yoga also became part of my investigation, because of serendipitous or perhaps Divine Intervention. One mother of my gymnastic peers was a yogini. She'd long dark hair and didn't shave anywhere. We went to the beach once and much to my embarrassment, much of her pubic hair seemed to escape from her one-piece bathing suit. Despite this she smelled **great,** sweet and syrupy, probably patchouli. I felt an affinity with her. She'd the gentlest and kind personality, and she intrigued me. She was different to most people I knew, ethereal almost.

Previously, a close friend of my father's left to become a sannyasin of Osho (then known as Bhagwan), leaving behind many of his possessions in our care. My sister, Melanie and I discovered one of his books, 'Yoga with Swami Sarasvati,' and so began my lifelong odyssey and errant pathway with yoga. Together we trialled many weird and wonderful shapes to put our lithe, flexible, and robust bodies into. The asana was incredible fun. We investigated different breathing techniques and tried various forms of meditation.

My gymnastics career came to an abrupt unscheduled finish when I had an accident practicing when I shouldn't have, waiting for Melanie's class to finish before mine began. I was attempting a complicated manoeuvre on the uneven bars. I was only supposed to practice with a coach spotting me. It concluded in me landing on my left arm and fracturing it. Despite having it medically re-broken twice, the doctors could never reset it properly, back into its original form. This meant I could utilise my arm in typical day-to-day activity, though it wasn't sufficient for the level of competition I'd reached. It didn't work in the same way as the right and nor was the alignment correct.

It crushed me. Gymnastics was my whole life. It was my Dream and my Passion. My 'tapas' (discipline), my santosha (contentment), my svadhyaya (self-study), my pratyhara (removal of senses from external to internal) and my Dharana (the practice of concentration). And I'd no one to blame for the incident but myself. I was full of recriminations and what-ifs. Which got me nowhere. In the end, it was the escapism option that beckoned and led me down another completely different path of experimentation and exploration - that of drugs and alcohol.

I also floated a little with yoga at my mum's suggestion.

"Mandi, why don't you come to yoga this week? Come to Margaret's class with me. Anyone can do yoga. It won't matter with your arm, it doesn't matter if you aren't in perfect alignment," she coaxed.

She was wise enough to see the road I was choosing wasn't good. A dead-end street where nothing grows.

I attended some classes, and did a little at home, realising the truth in my mother's words, but I was disheartened and had temporarily lost my tapas, my discipline. Any structured movement of my body was a bittersweet reminder of all I'd lost. It was much easier to run and hide in the external gratification of weekend parties, and burying of my 'self,' socialising with friends. The alternative was to explore and unravel the tight and growing ball of hurt with the compassion and forgiveness for which my heart ached.

You could say I 'dedicated' myself in earnest to my exploration with drugs over the next seven or eight years, traversing many frontiers with much excitement and gusto. Perhaps even discipline, though this would ignore an inherent meaning of tapas is 'purification through discipline', and there wasn't much sanctification in my scrutinization, more like pollution. That I was an experimentalist, was beyond a doubt.

A conversation as a twelve-year-old.

"Are you going to try drugs?" I asked a circle of friends at play lunch, curiously, as I had overheard a conversation the evening before about my aunty who was apparently using heroin. They all responded in the negative. Which was to be expected given we were a group of high achievers, both academically and athletically.

"What about you?" one of them asked.

"I am. I'm going to try everything once, and anything I like more," I stated.

My 'square' peers looked a little shocked. It was a bit out of character, though I was always a bit 'left field' and interested in investigating beyond the boundaries. There was just a bit of me that was undefinable, even as a schoolchild.

Tapas or discipline with my yogic 'sadhana' drifted in and out on a winding pathway over those eight years of destructive dissent, from age sixteen to twenty-four. Basically, I returned to union with my 'Self' whenever I had lost my way and needed the passage back to my Truth. And I always found this through the breath - 'pranayama' and meditation, eating healthily and movement - asana - yoga. This occurred recurrently between the ages of eighteen to forty. I would go through periods of dedicated, disciplined practice, then alternate the swing of the pendulum through to defilement and desecration. On the path for two weeks, one month, three months, six months, off the path for two weeks, one month, three months, six months. Practicing asana after a couple of drinks, after 'dropping' something.

Inherently, I knew what my body, mind and spirit most needed, though I was stubborn, carefree, and probably a bit stupid. The sheep-like mentality of society also pulled at me. It seemed insurmountable to maintain a healthy, Satvic life, full time, **even though** I knew instinctively and practically that was my ticket to journey home back to the essence of me.

It was only after I hit a real 'dead-end' finally, at forty I realised there was simply no other way for me. The truth had been with me since the beginning. I was to follow the path of yoga. This was my path of freedom. This was the path of exploration and experimentation. And this would require a lot of tapas. Of that, I had bucketloads.

Chapter Nine

THROUGH THE LOOKING GLASS, WHAT DO I SEE?

Svadhyaya

> "Patanjali's Yoga Sutra says:
> "Study thy self, discover the divine" II.44

Playlist - Omkara - Remember (Dec) 2008.

Find yourself a comfortable position and make your way to stillness. Step into the role of the observer to you. I like to imagine a part of myself standing beyond the body, beyond the mind with a pen and paper taking down notes like a scientist. Allow this, your journey back to Self to be the most excellent adventure. Be open to exploring the traverses of you with fresh eyes. Begin by being the witness to your Breath. Notice and appreciate the depth and pace of your breath. Without judgment, you are simply observing. Feel the coolness of the air as it comes in through the nostrils, the warmness as you expel it. Follow the breath's journey through the body. Oxygen in through the nostrils, through the sinuses, down through the trachea. Then into the lungs where it fills out the tiny sacs, and then follow its journey in reverse as the body releases the toxic waste, the carbon dioxide. Feel your belly rise and fall, observe the lungs, expand and contract. Notice any areas where your breath is catching.

Now let the breath go. Visualise from the crown of the head down to the tips of the fingers and the tips of the toes. Scan through your body with your powers of observation. Check in with those incredibly sacred and diligent parts that perform the holy work of storing and blocking energy on the rest of the system's behalf. We each have these points within our body. Perhaps it's around the eyes, through the forehead, the temples or the jaw, through the neck or a particular shoulder, the chest, the spine or anxiety through the stomach. Through your hips or your hamstrings, your knees or ankles. Wherever it is for you, observe that part of the body right now in this moment, and just simply detect **what** you are feeling.

Then **let** that go. Take your powers of perception, your conscious awareness to your thoughts, and observe where your mind is, observe your thoughts. Are you still caught up in earlier happenings of the day, or are you thinking about something that might happen in the future? If you are anywhere but **here** in this present moment, then perhaps visualise a silver sword cutting through the thoughts and repeat the following mantra in your mind after me. "**Be Here Now, Be Here Now, Be Here Now. I am here now. Be present with me**[7]."

This is the way I teach almost all of my yoga classes, followed by an acknowledgment of the Ancient Ones, the Ancestors and the Elders of the Country both Past and Present. It allows people the scope to connect in with themselves, right at the beginning. A reminder to observe the messages they will receive throughout the class and to create a stable, clear pathway to explore the rich travail of their inner world. For most of our lives, we are receiving information from the external world and processing that. Yoga is the golden gateway that presents the bridge to our Selves. It's

---

7. This is the same as a mindfulness practice https://youtu.be/M3S9JhqQj1E

integral to our process of involution, evolution, and self-understanding.

The physical practice, the asana, continues to develop the relationship to self and the method of observation. We take tree pose, Adho Mukha Vrksasana[8], for example, to the left and the right, and we notice which side is more in balance. We notice the line of our body, if there is a difference in the level or opening in each of the hips. And we observe the state of our mind and see if one side triggers a more emotional response than the other. We continue the Practice - sadhana - of observation or Svadhyaya - self-study. 'Sva' meaning self, 'Adhyaya', lesson, lecture or practice, off the mat and allow it free reign to overflow into the other realms of our lives. In many discussions surrounding the intention of Svadhyaya, some conjecture there are two 'selfs' to understand. The little 'self' relating to personality, body, mind, and the big 'Self' referring to the Essential Truth of who we are as Divine beings.

In our capacity of observers of our bodies, minds and external circumstances, we grant ourselves an opportunity to become more responsive and less reactive. We refine ourselves, and work towards growth and evolution. Before a dedicated practice, I was as reactive as the ball in a game of pinball, just bouncing and ricocheting from one landing or propulsion to the next. My asana practice, and meditation, plus the tapas and dedication to this, less the drugs and alcohol has allowed me an opportunity to be more mindful. I am *more* consciously aware, *less* triggered with much more concentration and focus to what is crucial for me and in the best interests of the Divine Self and Source. Though still a work in progress!

I have found growth and development of capital 'S.' 'Self' through many various opportunities, beyond my own mat, some more 'orthodox' than others. Attending yoga classes, workshops with Mark Whitwell, Shiva Rea, Ana Forrest, and Jose Calarco. Attending retreats and spiritual gatherings, women's circles with Alison Jarred, full moon drummings with John Whife. Sound healings with Julian Silburn, Satsang with

---

[8]. Adho Mukha Vrksasana - tree pose - link to demonstration https://youtu.be/IJROqcWcuHY

Beloved Mooji, Shanti Mayi, and various other gurus in India. I am a voracious reader. It is a regularity I have four to five books on the go, and I enjoy reading of all kinds of spiritual discourse. Some of my favourites are, Tibetan Book of the Dead, Autobiography of a Yogi, Bring Yoga to Life, Zen, and the Art of Motorcycle Maintenance. Also Bhagavad Gita, Patanjali's Yoga Sutras, Genekeys, and many other spiritual writings.

I have been fascinated by the 'spiritual' and esoteric path since I was a child bought up in an atheist household, asking to go to Sunday school with the neighbouring family. And I have flirted with most of the religious texts and been mesmerised by the world of gods and goddesses, mysticism, alchemy, saints, and sages. I learned to hold seances with a Ouija board at a young age with a drinking glass, cut out letters, and the support of my sister and cousins. I astral-travelled regularly as a child, exploring the terrains of timelines, and was enthralled with stories of ghosts, witches, dragons, nature spirits, and goblins.

One challenge I have found most difficult on my path is the lack of others walking an exact path as me. When I went off to yoga training, I was so excited as I thought I would meet so many others just like me. It turned out my spirituality was the path of separation. Likewise, amongst my 'spiritual' friends, my commitment to yoga and the sadhana is the path I walk alone. At age forty-five, almost five years into my journey of tapas, brahmacharya and saucha, my self-imposed austerity of freedom from alcohol and sexual activity, I tried something different. After much internal deliberation, I sat my first ayahuasca ceremony in the name of svadhyaya - of knowing myself better.

✳ ✳ ✳

I was lovingly gazing down at my new fire-engine red knee-high boots walking through the beach car-park with so much pride and admiration. I only noticed the dual cab four wheel drive as it hit me. It happened so quickly. I was on my way to my friend's birthday dinner, running my obligatory ten minutes late. I felt the car collide with me. I was propelled a little airborne, then miraculously landed on both feet, unharmed. Immediately, I rushed up to the driver, as he held his face in his hands, checking to see if he was okay. He was almost crying.

"Oh shit," he blubbered. "Are you okay?"

He was attempting to manoeuvre an iPhone out of my viewpoint. I was given the impression he'd been texting or trying to put a song through the stereo, so his attention had been elsewhere too.

"I'm fine," I said. "Completely fine." I laid a hand on his arm. "But are you okay?"

"Are you sure? F**k I can't believe I just hit you. I wasn't paying attention. I'm so sorry. Oh My God!"

"It's okay," I reassured him. "It's okay. I'm honestly **okay**, which I'm finding difficult to believe because you did just hit me, but I'm okay."

We continued the same theme for a couple more minutes, then after reassuring him, finally, I walked off, observing my body for any feeling of injury. It felt completely fine. Perhaps a slight 'something' on my right leg and hip that had taken the impact, but on the whole, all okay. Actually, so okay that as I walked off, I began to doubt my perception of reality. I began to wonder if it had happened at all or had been a figment of my imagination.

"Oh My God. Are you okay?" A complete stranger, a woman in her mid-30s, came rushing out of a restaurant to ask.

"Oh, did you see that?" I asked, partially in relief. "I was wondering if it had happened, because the funny thing is that I am, very **okay**," I reassured her.

"I didn't believe what I saw," the lady continued incredulously. "He hit you, and you just walked up to the car."

"Well, that makes two of us," I laughed. "Thank you so much for coming up to me because I might not have believed it happened without you doing so."

"I hope you are okay," she said.

"I am, thank you again." I smiled and brushed her arm as I walked off.

***

I had twenty-four hours to ponder this event before sitting in a sacred ceremony the next day, and it helped me to form my Sankalpa or intention for the journey. Because of my interest in the 'unknown,' my experience with death, and my mum's passing a year prior, my intention for the 'medicina' was a request to explore the realms of death.

The drink was bitter, very difficult to swallow, and I sat in a room with about fifty others as I waited for the effects of taking place. An experienced Shaman held space with his chosen assistants anchoring each of the directions. Despite my natural fear of the unknown, I felt as safe as I could. They'd instructed us to have a clean 'diet' for the past four days so the medicine could have full effect and not interact with anything else. For me, basically this meant to avoid that sneaky piece of chocolate I might furtively consume as I had continually been refining and purifying my body over the past five years. Combined with the amount of hot yoga I took part in and therefore sweated; I was pretty much crystalline.

Thirty minutes later, amongst the 'icaros,' the particular songs sung to guide the journey, I started to feel a little like labour at the point the baby is about to come. Not pain, rather I'd changed my mind, and no longer thought this was a good idea. I wanted to leave the building and go home. I felt all I was losing, and that was my present reality. I had to release my attachments to that and all I'd known. I didn't want to. Then it was too late. Way too late. I gazed at my two hands, the left becoming larger.

I don't want to do this anymore, I thought in fear.

"Too late, dear, you've invited me in," said Mother Aya.

And then the journey began. To begin with, it was carnival-like, full of psychedelics, like tripping on acid, liquorice all-sort craziness, and I wanted escapism from this, I was so full of dread. I was thinking, if I'd known it would be like this I never would have gone there. I left drugs and acid behind so many years ago. I didn't want to come back here.

I was full of remorse and dread. I felt I'd lost everything I'd worked towards over the past five years and regretted my decision to journey with Ayahuasca. I was caught in it at that point though. The only thing to do was breathe, the only way out being through. The journey continued, and the Mother, the name she is known by, showed me the meaning of my journey here over the past twenty-four hours.

In an alternate reality, the car hit me, and I died.

Not realising, I'd rushed around trying to find a suit for my son who had a ball coming up, trying to find some shoes for my daughter and tying up other loose ends.

But 'I' didn't exist anymore.

She showed me a hospital room with me in the bed, but it wasn't me it was just my body. She showed how previously I'd been removed from the scene of the accident, red-legged boots splayed on the bitumen road. The devastated driver, crying, being taken away in handcuffs, getting into a police car. And the lady from the restaurant talking to other police about what she'd witnessed, mascara running down her wet face. My friends who I was meeting for the birthday dinner, outside in a huddle, crying.

Then me in the ambulance, face covered. Flashes to my kids being given the news. My dad hearing about it. Their non- belief and devastation. An understanding I'd indeed 'passed' in that accident. At this point I wondered if it, in fact, was the truth. The feeling of futility was thick for me as I viewed this and a degree of responsibility.

I felt if I hadn't called in the Aya experience, no one would be dealing with my death right now.

The next vision was of my mum's death and her journey. Then it flicked back to my journey as I died and issues with attachments to my kids, and my dog, which kept me connected to this earthly experience. A deep understanding that for 'me' to rise from the body, and into the next realm, I needed to let go of my ties to my attachments - Aparigraha.

Eventually, I let go, and I found myself in a vast and dark corridor. At the end was a door to be opened. Beyond the door was an endless room without borders with everyone dressed in white. I looked down and saw I was in white too. We were all like saints or something. She guided me to 'my spot' in amongst many others. There was a massive crystal 'scrying ball' in front of me, and I watched a film about my life unravel before my eyes. She showed me the crucial moments from all perspectives, not just my own. All-encompassing, and all-knowing, my scope moved beyond my personal experience to incorporate that of all. It was an empathic, bird's-eye view of deep understanding of my journey and experiences until this point, including those who played roles within them, from their frame of reference. A little like looking upon the single-crystal though seeing the different fractals 'faces' of it all at the same time.

There were sounds of people crying around me. Some in absolute remorse and devastation they hadn't understood the true meaning of life wasn't to accumulate as much as we could. It was to love as much as we could. I watched my life story flashing before my eyes. I felt infinite love and compassion for the person I watched and slightly detached as if I were my best friend - a clear practice of ahimsa.

Next scene I found myself sitting around a campfire with many poncho-clad Elders, grey-haired faces, deeply etched dry riverbeds. They sang songs, and there was a feeling of movement around us, movement across time and space. We were calling the next soul into the vortex. From far, far away, out of clouds of gas and dust, a cosmic event unfolding, the stars were giving birth through the elements of the hydrogen, helium, phosphorous, carbon and nitrogen. Through the disbursement, the next body would be birthed.

This campfire was the last stopping point before re-incarnation. I felt I had been here many times before. I felt myself take a deep breath, and I landed back in the living body I'd left in the hospital. I knew immediately all would be okay. The machines indicated I was breathing. I'd survived being hit by the car while I was lovingly gazing upon my red boots. Aya provided another alternate reality, and direct and complex experiences of attachment, non-attachment, and rebirth.

The second cup of medicine was offered, but I was content with the first. I felt fulfilled. I didn't need it anymore. I had a deep respect for what had been Gifted through the journey. It was enough. Santosha.

This was a very portent experience for me, offering an insight into what may happen as we pass. This new-found knowledge comforted me. It had resonance and sat well with me. Mother Aya had served me well.

I utilised parts of this experience in a 'death meditation' that I teach. It gives people the opportunity for rebirth and to view their life with fresh eyes, perhaps re-prioritising what is essential to them and re-shuffling where it's required. Some people get angry with me for 'killing' them, others appreciate the sagacity in what it offers. My ayahuasca journey allowed me an insight into death and rebirth I would not have otherwise had. This allowed me knowledge of the importance of living a life expressing what made my spirit and the Divine soar, so there would be no recriminations or lamentations at the end. A further realisation was a reinforcement of the commitment I'd made to my children. Every 'Aya' journey is considered a mini-death. It was not something I would enter again lightly. In fact, I doubt many people enter medicine journey's lightly, and if they do, then they are utterly foolish. It is by not a recreational drug, to be taken 'willy nilly'. It is a doorway into another reality, offering rich, painful and beautiful knowledge. Mother Aya doesn't 'behave', if I dare say that, as a drug anyhow. If you drop an MDMA or speed, it will affect anyone, whereas Aya will only meet you if you are prepared to 'drop' and meet her. She is a 'consciousness,' and not one to ingest lightly. I have heard some people have to have five or more cups, and still, they don't 'drop' because they cannot allow their consciousness to meet her. They are waiting for it to simply 'happen' as you would when you take recreational or prescribed drugs. Ayahuasca is a plant consciousness- she has her own identity- and this is not to be confused with chemical drug use. Should you find your interest piqued by reading this chapter, ensure that you only follow through in sitting in Sacred Space with a **very** experienced shaman. It is not worth putting the rest of your life in jeopardy by journeying with those not capable or skilled enough to hold a safe, secure space for you.

***

Conclusively, to gain knowledge about yourself, be prepared to explore. And you have to be prepared that sometimes you won't like what you find. Most often than not, the 'hard-truths' about ourselves are the most difficult to bear, though acceptance of these also provides the pathway to liberation. The mind may perceive your discovery to be an 'awkward' acknowledgment about the self to admit to the Self, let alone anyone else or publicly. It takes courage and strength to honestly look at yourself, confronting your shadows, your wounds, and weaknesses, to reveal the masks that band-aid our self-perception and provide such proficient operating systems. A tool I've found beneficial in understanding myself better and learning about this temple I inhabit is through Richard Rudd's Genekeys. (www.Genekeys.com) And in the jewels presented daily - what I discover in my asana or meditation sadhana. As well as mirrored within my close personal relationships.

In a journey of self-discovery, like any pilgrimage we undertake, we need to ensure we have the right supplies for what we may encounter. A sense of direction (compass), a willingness to flesh things out (some food to sustain us) and fluidity (water) to sustain the body and the mind. Only the baggage we can easily carry. A willingness to experience and perhaps embrace new things, letting go of the old and out-dated. To definitely be open to observation, and this is what lies at the heart of Svadhyaya. The ultimate exploration and evolution of the Self.

Chapter Ten

I SURRENDER

Isvara pranidhana

Playlist - Ben Harper - I'll Rise 1994

Of all the Sanskrit words, Ishvara pranidhana is definitely one of my favourites. I love the way it rolls off the tongue. Try it. Ish - vara Pra – ni - dhana. It means to surrender to a higher power than ourselves, to dedicate and devote our lives to the Divine, to God. It requires we let go of our ego and personality demands, our need to be in control. To simply, 'Let go and Let God' or 'Let go and Let Love.' Despite sounding very easy, from a Westerner's perspective, it can be challenging. At a basic level as a child, I remember quarrels along these lines.

"You stole my lolly," I said to Melanie.

"Did not," she declared.

"Did too."

"Did not."

"Did too."

"Did not."

"Did too."

"Did not."

"Did tooooooooooooo. GIVE IT BACK."

Etcetera, Etcetera. Declaring our stance. Unwilling to compromise or to see another possibility. I'd decided what the reality was, and my sister rightfully or wrongfully - who knows if she took my lolly, defended her own conscience or truth. Inevitably this would have led to violence. I probably would have pushed her over or something, and then we would have wrestled. Not indifferent to what occurs at a fundamental level when we defend our 'rights', our point of view with another. In most situations, what we are trying to do is to force our point of view down another's throat, because our version is 'correct' and theirs isn't. There is no winner in this, nor Love. It is merely a mechanism of Power and Control.

***

I lived in Broome when I was eighteen and held a 'death of a teenager' celebration for my twentieth birthday. It was my first time really away from home, some twenty-four hours by bus, two thousand, two hundred and fifty kilometres away. I was there after impatience in waiting with a friend for a mining job to come through in another far northern town, Karratha. I had gone for a weekend visit to Broome and decided that was where I wanted to be, close to the sea. I was still youthfully experimenting with alcohol and recreational drugs, mainly ecstasy, exploring and enjoying the realms of freedom in most spheres.

I loved Broome, the multicultural society, the sultry weather, sweet and juicy fruits. And I loved its soulful sunsets, the majestic cyan colour of the sea reflecting off the endless fine white sand of low tide. Earthed in the centre by ruby rich pindan earth, rust red, it carried stories deep in the heart of Gaia. It was a land like no other, abundant with the Ancient history of Dreamtime and No Time. It whispered sweet somethings to my spirit, etching, and imprinting love letters upon my soul, each day frangipani petals that unfurled magically to unfold.

I was blessed to have many jobs while I lived there, working for car-rental companies and in hospitality. I experimented with some modelling and gained a little notoriety. I was in a relationship with a quirky pearl diver, Brent, eight years my senior. We shared his small room in a rental share house with three others even while he was out working on the sea. When he came back in after a 'swing' of sea time of twelve days or so, he was all cashed up, looking to party and up for having a good time. This usually meant lots of alcohol and some 'eccies.' (ecstasy) Which made for lots of fun times with little sleep. Most of the guys off the boats ran a similar lifestyle, and the local pubs, taxis and restaurants loved it when the Divers were back in town.

Incongruently, yet simultaneously, Brent was also very dedicated to his health and eating the 'correct' food, fasting for lengths of time, and he diligently practiced daily yoga and meditation. So, his influence upon me traversed both the positive and the negative poles. It was a pleasurable, relatively easy-going time in my life as I played with my newly found independence from parental scrutiny. Finally, the long-held 'leash' from childhood was off. No one knew me up there. I was free to be who I chose. There was no history, and no one held me to any expectations. A perfect opportunity to allow me the time to discover me.

***

In the year of my 'death of a teenager' party, Brent and I prepared to visit my family in Perth via Bali for Christmas. At the beginning of December, one hotel held an early fancy dress Christmas celebration for their staff. I went scantily clad as a Genie. Black baggy see-through hessian style pants and an itty bitty bra top. There was a stairwell to climb before you got up to the bar where I was employed, and this was where the function was being held. A large, spacious room, your eyes immediately are drawn and feasting upon the most magnificent view of infinite turquoise water. I raced up the stairwell, keen to join my co-workers, apparently unforgivably forgetting to greet the hotel hired bouncers who manned these steps.

Drink and cigarettes in hand, I socialised and danced with my friends, celebrating and excitedly chatting about my upcoming trip to Bali and back home to take Brent to 'meet the parents'. I remember little of the party past the second drink. I'm not even sure I had another drink. I was not a particularly 'good' drinker. I was partial to extending myself beyond my limits to explore further landscapes. My memory was never usually impaired after two drinks though. My last memories of being in the bar are of dancing and having fun, talking with the bouncers, and my friends and then all I have is blackness.

Then out of the abyss, my arms and legs are pinned down by four hands, two of the bouncers and one is thrusting his way inside of me. I feel their hot, excited breath infiltrating my cells as much as I feel the invasion of an unwanted weapon. I try to squirm, but there is no moving. Looking up past his face, I realise I am in a hotel room of the establishment. My eyes widen in terror, and then I surrender to the pummelling and to the situation. There is nowhere to go and nothing else to do. I disassociate from my body and my mind. I am above the scene watching dispassionately, disconnected from the events. I feel nothing because I am not that body and I am not that mind. From this perspective, I see Brent open the door. I see his eyes widen, then in cowardice, realising the futility of his smallness concerning their size, I see him gently close the door and skulk away. He doesn't come back with help like I might have hoped. Any part of me still within that human body has now retracted into spirit form, to the stars and greater cosmos above. The body, the mind, the personality called Mandi remains on the bed being fucked in whichever way the men choose. But I am not she. I exist beyond this. And where I am, they cannot reach me.

They each have a turn and leave Mandi on the bed.

The next morning just after 8.30am I wake up splayed across the bed, sheets crumbled, jumbled and spread. For a moment I forget, and I am surprised to be in a hotel room at the Mangrove and think 'wow I must have got drunk last night.' Then I go to move, and my soul shatters into a thousand pieces as the bruises of my assaulted body scream to make themselves heard. I feel a pool of wetness between my legs, sour smell, and all at once feel nauseous. My mind flashes to a vision of being held down and raped, and I immediately retract and let it go. Confining the memory to a space where I can live with my sanity intact. Locked up tightly in a deep dark corner of my mind. I search across the room for my clothing, scattered and strewn, and gingerly make my way to have a quick shower. Then I re-dress and go into the kitchen to get them to organise a taxi for me.

"Good morning," I announce with forced cheerfulness, interrupting a conversation, my voice cracking a little. "How are we all? Can you guys call me a taxi?"

"Hey, Mandi are you okay?" asks the chef, Peter, stepping away from the food he was cooking, and turning to face me squarely. He was always such a sensitive and caring soul.

"Yeah, I'm fine, what a night!" I answer brushing off his concern, keeping my memories safely locked away. I will not surrender to this emotion.

"No, Mandi, I mean, are you **all right**?" he implores as he moves to place a hand on my forearm.

I sense he **knows** and there is **no way** I am going there. I don't know how he knows, but from the way he is acting, there is little doubt for me that I was. That it happened. I'm filled with shame and don't know where to look. I avoid his eyes and look down.

"Yeah, I'm fine." I hold back a sob. "I just need to get home. I'm sure Brent will be worried about where I've been all night."

"Are you sure that's what you want?" he implores. "There is nowhere else you might like to go. The hospital, police?"

"No, seriously, I'm fine, I just need a taxi," I plead, my eyes downward cast.

Peter shares a look with the apprentice and a nod, and the apprentice, Derek, takes over Peter's pan.

"Okay then, I'm giving you a lift," he states.

There is no room for movement, and I do not have the energy to argue anyway. I am grateful. "Thank you," I respond while giving him a look that is reproachful, telling him with my look I will accept his lift but want no more of that conversation.

Where I live is only a couple of minutes away, so I am spared more conversation, aside from banal general questions. Peter has understood my unspoken request. As I gingerly get out of the car he softly says, "Take it easy, kid. You know if you need anything, just shout out."

"I'll be fine," I say brushing his softness off, afraid it will open the part of my heart I've padlocked and vaulted from sight. "Thanks for the lift," I falter.

His car drives off, and I make my way into the house, to the kitchen. To make a 'cuppa' and brace myself to deal with Brent. Brent is already in the kitchen and demands, "Where were you last night?"

"Oh, I got pretty drunk pretty early, so they put me in a hotel room," I stated matter-of-fact. I kept my face turned towards the kettle, away from his so he couldn't read anything else.

"Good night was it?" he asks.

"Yep, not bad," I state.

"Anything interesting happen?" Brent says, fishing.

"Nah just the usual, you know." I'm making my instant coffee, trying to deflect.

"So, who stayed in the room then? Was it just you?"

"Yep, just me. I was pretty drunk. I passed out," I turn to make my way out of the room.

"Lying slut, I saw you. Did they make you f**k them too?" his words commanded.

Memory rushes back from where I'd locked it up. I see him opening the door and then sneaking back out again. I simultaneously lash out at him, and my voice cracks. "You were there, you saw…" Incredulously, "How could you walk in and **not** do anything?" I demanded. It sickened me to the stomach; my legs gave way. I wanted the ground to open up and swallow me. The barrage of images unrolling and unravelling through my mind were way too much to bear. I slid my way down the kitchen cupboards, head in hands.

"I walked in and saw you fucking three guys," he justified.

"You walked in and saw me being gang-raped by three guys and chose not to do anything about it," I seethed and spat. I was both demonically mad and infinitely sad at the same time. "And you call yourself my f**cking boyfriend?" I moaned, curled myself up into a ball and began to sob my bleeding heart all over the kitchen floor. I had cracked, and once more, I surrendered. I surrendered to the emotion and the flow of the suffering that needed to be expelled so I might find some healing somewhere and somehow.

Brent let me go for a bit and then came over and placed a hand on my back, repeatedly telling me how sorry he was, could I forgive him? He was crying too.

The next week before our scheduled trip to Bali passed in a gin-haze as more people realised what happened. They came to sit on the frangipani-bloomed bull-nosed veranda, to drink, to offer their support. They gave me so many bottles of gin. The local police came to see if I wanted to lay charges. I didn't see the point. I was wearing next to nothing, I was drunk, possibly drugged, and this was in the late eighties. There was no way I would win the case. Besides, I'd decided to leave town. My Broome days were over, so it didn't matter.

I had surrendered, but the girl, a former model I lived with, had not. She got in touch with her a friend from 'another life' who was fairly high up in an outlawed motorcycle gang. He sent up some 'boys' who dealt with the men who'd 'dealt' with me. I heard that there were some broken bones, and some of the guys ended up hanging around they liked the place so much.

Ishvara Pranidhana asks that we let go of our need to control outcomes and events and let them play out by themselves. To let go and let love or to let go and let God in.

Chapter Eleven

THEY SURRENDERED

Ishvara Pranidhana

Playlist – Paul Kelly and Kev Carmody - From Little Things Big Things Grow 1993

It took me a long time to put that experience to rest, to fully let go. I did lots of healing work and counselling over many years to come to a place of forgiveness and acceptance. There were many Lessons and therefore Gifts in that outplay. Perhaps the greatest was the opportunity to be in a position where I had been a 'victim' and then to move beyond the blaming, to accept my responsibility in it. From there, I found my way to the path of forgiving myself and the men involved.

It took a while, but eventually, I found more 'functional' means to 'deal' with the experience, rather than blocking or using drugs or alcohol. Through being able to let it go, I reclaimed my power. It no longer pulled strings from behind the scene. I was no longer a puppet to this event. This is the magic unfolding in letting go. In our vulnerability, we find our strength. In hearing the Call to take Higher Ground, we can find our way back to Love and Acceptance.

The First Nations People of Australia know this situation very well. As a people, I'm ashamed from a Caucasian perspective that it's like they have been 'gang-raped' by the white invasion of their land and attempt to eradicate their culture. They have experienced genocide in many forms over the years and have had no choice but to practice 'Ishvara pranidhana' if they wanted to stay alive. They have had to let go of the ego, which they have, and are exemplary examples of humbleness. These people are the oldest living culture still surviving on the planet, yet they are treated by most Australians, either overtly or covertly as the lowest echelon of society in Australia. The lowest of lows. Fancy that! Those who we could learn the most from all over the planet, here on the land we live on and they are treated like the Scum of the Earth. The racism is that interwoven within our fabric to most it is invisible.

I became passionate about the 'First Nations People Cause,' offering my time (sometimes **lots** of time) on a direct dial-up from Spirit. When I made my commitment to my 'ten year experiment' I also made the conscious choice to notice the little messages Spirit is always giving each of us. To tune into those - goose bumps - which I refer to as 'god bumps': to follow the signs in nature. To take notice of the bird that flew past the car, its species, to take heed of its message. And to **act** upon each of these communications that felt 'right' or resonated for me. To use these as my compass to navigate life, surrendering to the flow that unfolded, allowing my body to be an instrument of the Divine Will.

One of 'those' forms the stem of where **all** of my relationships with Aboriginal people flower from; on a Spirit-led impulse on a Saturday night in late 2012, to respond to a First Nations Person I didn't even know. He had come upon someone else's feed on social media, 'Joe Collard' and posted about needing someone to assist with some media work.

The urge to respond was so intense through my body I didn't even have time to blink my eyes. I'd already typed and fired off my response. Then I sat bewildered over what happened. I was not in the practice of messaging random men, Aboriginal or otherwise. It seemed Spirit was behind this one. Dumbstruck, I couldn't pull it back. Now I waited. And waited.

It took 'Joe Collard' a while to respond.

After my initial excitement, my heart gave a little leap. A sure sign from Spirit I'm moving in the right direction. But each time I heard the notification go off on my iPhone, only to be disappointed, I turned my thoughts and focus to other things.

In the Collective Consciousness, the interplay where the thought-form had originated from was already manifesting, another 'thought' formed. It would get picked up by Joe, who would turn it into form and put some impetus into that on the twentieth, 2012. Mid-morning as I was 'driving up the hill,' on an hour journey, I had an urge to put the radio on.

I was on my way for the first time to meet a new spiritual community in the windy roads of Mundaring. I was feeling a little excited about what would unfold. Alison Jarred had arranged to have a well-known Aboriginal woman, a Larrakia Elder from the Northern Territory on her and husband Graeme's property, in their Tipi for the auspicious date of twenty-first December 2012. This was the date referred to by the Mayan people, whereby their calendar came to a close. They and many other indigenous Elders from across the planet prophesied this particular date heralded an end to the times of Power and Corruption, and the beginning of the movement to unity conscious or 'one-ness'. As an extension of this sentiment, Alison and Graeme created an event for Perth people to attend and lend their intentions to upon their property. And as an extension of that Bilawarra, offered to do a women-only sitting the day before. I'd seen this on Facebook and sent Alison a message asking if I could come to take some photos. They'd given me permission, and here it was. I was excited to see what unfolded over the next two days.

I switched on the radio and out came the twang of a mouth harmonica and the strum of two unplugged acoustic guitars. Then came the voices of all-time favourite folk Australian musician, Paul Kelly, and First Nation's Person, Kev Carmody. They shared the story of British Lord Vestey and Aboriginal Vincent Lingiarri and Vincent's fight to get his land back in the iconic song, 'From Little Things, Big Things Grow'. I got covered in god bumps, another confirmation that Spirit was directing or encouraging me to continue on the path I was on. Then while the song was playing I got a Facebook notification sound on my phone. I looked across and saw it was from Joe Collard. *Right at that moment.* I got god bumps on top of god bumps. It was feeling like a rush of energy, rolling up and down my body, all over my face and ears. Entranced, I pulled my car over for a minute. It was an exquisite feeling, goose bumps rolling up and down my body and face, while on the radio was still playing the last verse.

I totally, absolutely, unequivocally, without a doubt, **knew** I was following the right path. The signs could not have been more manifest. Joe's message to me was basically just asking when I wanted to meet up to chat. The synchronic timing of this message reminded me of what I had read about the Australian Aboriginals. They're famous for their capacity of playing within Dreamtime - being able to be both in the forward and the backward time. This was the first time **ever** I was even going to anything that was remotely 'Aboriginal'. His timing was implicit, and I knew Spirit wanted me to work with him, whatever he was talking about. It was inspiring, affirmative, and incredibly exhilarating.

I really enjoyed those couple of days I spent with wise medicine woman, Bilawarra Lee, in the Tipi with Alison and it led to many associations of mutual affection. Bilawarra imparted some infinite wisdom about the 'day,' connecting it with Aboriginal knowledge from the stars.

Joe and I started communicating off and on, via messenger intermittently though we didn't catch up until early January 2013, at a commercial burger place in the city. I felt I was being 'tested' by him. I didn't think he trusted me to begin with. And to be fair, I'm not sure I trusted him. I had to make my way through a lifetime of my own 'judgment' around the First Nations People, the racism I'd been bought up with and stay in my heart. To remind myself I trusted Spirit though, and that's how this was set up.

I remember that first meeting. Joe was there with another Aboriginal male friend, sitting at a table. Recognising me from my Facebook profile pic I guess, he called me over, motioning with my hand. He is roughly my height, a little taller, a little more rotund than me. I check in to his energy field and felt nothing threatening there. I feel as if I am being 'checked out' too.

"Gya Mandi," spoke Joe. "This is Brendon. Say hi Brendon."

"Hey," I said.

"Hi," Brendon muttered with a cursory glance at me as he continued to play on his phone.

"So, you got gear, right?" Joe asked.

I was taking all of him in. He'd dressed in a pair of black sporty style tracksuit pants with the white line running down the side, Adidas shoes and a black t-shirt. He was a good-looking man, reasonably fit, though bordering on the point where he needed to make drastic dietary and lifestyle changes or deal with the consequences. His smile projected joy at a thousand wattage, though it seemed he was a little shy and wouldn't hold my gaze for so long.

"Yes, I have all the gear. We can even record separate sound if you want too," I declared.

"Right, and what about editing then? Can you do that too?" he asked.

I watch mesmerised as droplets of sweat are rolling from his chocolate-brown, bulbous bald forehead, following its path down some sort of gang tattoo on his neck as we speak. He is hot or nervous too. At least he only has to deal with me.

"Yeah, I have editing software. It's not my favourite thing to do, but I can do it. If there's any money we can get someone else to do it," I suggested.

"There's not any money."

"Oh." I had a feeling this was being done in Seva - the Sanskrit word for service, so it didn't really surprise me. "What is it actually that you want to be filmed?"

"I want you to follow me around talking to people about Native Title," Joe stated.

I'd heard about Native Title - Land Rights, so this was big.

"What about Native Title?" I asked, composed, and intrigued.

"What do you know about Native Title?" Joe bounced back.

"Not much really. There's not that much in the papers - even if I read them. I'll have to google."

"Mandos, there's not much at all that tells our side of the story **or** different perspectives that you will find anywhere. That's why we gotta do what we gotta do," Joe explained.

"Okay," I agreed, thinking I'm googling when I get home.

"It's about the Alternative Settlement Deal," Joe expanded as he slurped on a large commercial coke that turned my stomach. I wanted to tell him how bad that was for him but stopped myself. It was our first meeting.

"What's that?" I ventured.

"The government is trying to push its way onto our land. We got a Native Title Claim already in the High Court, probably take another twenty years to go, yeah. They wanna bring it forward, divide up our land, divide up our people, pay us money to sell it off. Call it Alternative Settlement Deal," he added.

I noticed his skin looked as if it would be really soft to touch.

"Okay, so am I getting it right? You don't wanna sell your land, you're happy to wait, but they are pushing you to sell? Why would they do that?" I asked, trying to figure it out.

"Property Development," we both said.

"So why don't I know about this? This sux. Why isn't it in the papers or on the news?"

"Have a think about that one, Mandi. You prob don't see much about Aboriginal people unless it's about them getting into trouble," Joe explained.

Even though I wasn't reading the papers, I knew the truth when I heard it.

"So, there is a deal on the table that we don't want, that we didn't ask for, that they are pushing us all to be a part of. It gives us the worst pockets of land; we don't even get the one point three billion they are talking about. That's an imaginary figure because it's only that if it's compound by interest and we never touch it. Besides, **we** cannot sell our land because **we** are the custodians of the land. It's part of our spirituality and our culture. We sell our land, **we** get sick. Break connection to land, break our spirit," said Joe, slurping the bottom of his coke.

I was on a steep learning curve. This was all news to me. I'd done my research on Joe Collard. He held a degree in a Bachelor of Science in Indigenous Community Management and Development Practitioner and a Diploma in Linguistics in the Northern Territory. I was inclined to take his word verbatim.

"So, we are going to go around and get people to talk about what their point of view is. At the moment there is just one voice getting out to my people, and it's the government's. They have a big budget, paying people off to say what they want them to say. So, you and I right, we going to go around and film some people with some different opinions on this."

"Okay, I'll do some research," I suggested.

"I already know who we are going to film. You just have to follow me around," Joe expanded, pushing his cup away.

"Okay, so when do we start?" I asked, a little excited.

"Soon, soon, soon. I'll let you know when the time is right." He got up from the plastic chair. "Come on, Brendon, time to go."

And that was it. It was done.

"See ya, Mandox." (His nickname for me.)

"Bye Joe, Brendon."

"Say goodbye Brendon. He doesn't have many brain cells. His mum suffered while she was while pregnant. Sorry business," he explained.

"Bye," said Brendon.

***

Over the next couple of weeks, we caught up a couple of times at various spots around the city. Joe was never by himself. I learned why later. Most times it was Brendon with him, sometimes his kids. Then I received an invitation to come to watch his son play soccer for the Perth Glory youth squad. I went, and he gave me a 'messenger stick.'

"This is so we can communicate now," he explained.

I was a little perplexed about how that would happen being the high-tech multimedia advocate I was, though understood there was a reverence attached. It kind of felt like I was 'in'. Message sticks are ancient ways of communication in the Aboriginal world. I felt quite chuffed to get one. It is still one of my most prized possessions. I didn't understand how it was to be used, but that didn't matter. It seemed an honour.

We finally managed filming the week after Joe gave me the message stick. I still wasn't sure what I was doing. Plus, this was my first documentary too. I was feeling a little out of my depth, but I liked Joe. I felt connected to him in some way. And I trusted Spirit. We went to numerous locations, across the city, including Dumbartung, Aboriginal Legal Service, South West Aboriginal Land, and Sea Council. We spoke to various Aboriginal Elders and leaders, getting all of their perspectives on the proposed deal on the table. I met lots of genuine, passionate, articulate, and grateful people, for the work we were doing on the film. And this was how I also met my beloved Nanna Violet.

After the filming came the editing, and what an arduous task that was. So many hours of footage to go through. Time was of the essence, the voting was coming up soon, and Joe wanted to put our film out there before then, so people understood there were other options. I also needed Joe to be a part of it all as I still wasn't one hundred percent sure what he wanted. We edited for about eight weeks. I just had to focus on the film and let go of any other opportunities to work and therefore became 'on the bones of my arse' financially.

It was another practice of 'Ishvara pranidhana.' I just needed to surrender and trust the process. The last time money was this lacking was in my early Margaret River days, and as a university student. I had to go into my kid's catholic schools and speak to either the head of finance or the headmaster and tell them their fees would have to wait. I was in the middle of doing a film, voluntarily, to assist the Aboriginal People. Then Joe would turn up to edit with a couple of 'extras' in tow, and I would feed them all.

My affection for Joe began to deepen. I learned he'd a cheeky sense of humour and was knowledgeable about Aboriginal culture and Nyungar language. We worked together well. Neither of us was afraid to 'argue' our point of view, so editing was lively and full of laughter.

Somewhere through this process, as our film "Displaced Voices" began to crystallise into a form from the recesses of my lounge room, I began to wonder about my heritage. My skin colour had always been 'olive,' tanning up really well in the sun. There'd been whisperings on my dad's side of the family that perhaps there was some Aboriginal blood too. This is because of us being here so long in Australia. We arrived close to when the first fleet did.

There are so many stories in Australia, of people who were half Aboriginal and never knew, and only found out years later. Or they pretended they weren't Aboriginal to be saved from being forcibly taken away to be raised in the missions, in what has been termed the 'stolen generation'. The prevalence of white men either raping or taking 'liberties' with the Aboriginal women upon their land was rife. There were so many literal skeletons in any family closet. And it had been whispered there was some in ours too. I decided I wanted to know.

One night I started to dig online through ancestry.com. I wanted to see what I could find, and part of me was secretly hoping to discover I was Aboriginal. I'd such a kinship with Joe. I felt like he was my brother or something. I really felt for the Aboriginal cause. And after spending time with him, I'd an indication of the racism that was an atrocious part of his day-to-day life. Things like shutting the petrol pump down and Joe having to prepay his fuel while everyone else at the petrol station was paying afterward. The harsh unmitigated looks of disdain as we entered an eating establishment. The beady eyes watching every move as we made our way through a shopping centre, and security even tailing us one day. I say if you want to tell me racism doesn't exist in Australia, hang out with an Aboriginal for a day. Then let's talk.

What I unravelled in my research that evening just about dismantled me. Through various means and search engines, I spiralled my way through the rabbit hole. I traced my ancestral lines to discover I was related to an Irish man named 'John Smith' (1795 - 1862), a 'colour sergeant' of the Twenty-first regiment and my Fourth paternal great grandfather. He was first shown in Australian records to have been on the ship 'Portland' docked initially in Hobart on the fourth of July 1833. He made his way with his wife and children to settle in Perth aboard the 'Isabella.' I was utterly gobsmacked to uncover he was also a part of the Pinjarra Massacre. It is said that fifteen to twenty aboriginal men and an unknown amount of women and children were murdered. I was floored, like someone dropped me from a hundred-floor skyscraper splattered across the ground. I felt sickened to my stomach that I could have this man's blood within me. I went to bed sick to my soul. I felt a deep shame, horror and guilt that I could be related to someone capable of that behaviour.

I stayed out of touch with Joe for a couple of days while I allowed time for this new reality to settle. I spent a lot of the time feeling nauseous. My heart physically felt like there was a gaping wound within it, jagged, stretch and torn. I felt self-loathing and disgust. My bed seemed to be a mammoth black cavern of infinite despair. I was finding it difficult to pull myself out of bed. I was feeling this so deeply, at a soul level. After the third day, I realised Joe needed to know, and I had to tell him I could no longer work on the film. I felt I'd no right to do so and my involvement would sully the project. I phoned him.

"Joe?"

"Gya Nganya djoog, Noonaa Boolg. Translation, Hello my sister. You are a champion woman," Joe greeted me.

I swallowed. "I have to tell you something, Joe."

"What's that, my babiny?" he said. (friend)

"I did some researching a couple of nights back, some digging on my family history. You know I told you it's always been said we have some Aboriginal blood somewhere right?"

"Mmm, yeah I think you have said that," Joe said.

"Well, I wanted to find out. It's not what I thought though." I took an intense deep inhalation. "What I found was my fourth great grandfather was part of the Pinjarra Massacre." Pause. "I feel incredibly sick. I have barely been able to leave my bed since I discovered. I just **cannot** believe I have this man's blood running in my veins," I managed to get out.

"True," said Joe.

"Yes," I said.

"Ahh, sorry business. I lost some of my family in that massacre, right?" Joe said quietly.

It was worse than I thought.

"Oh My God. Joe, I'm so sorry. I want to apologise on behalf of my ancestor's actions," I broke. "I am just so sorry. I cannot believe I am related to someone like that."

"That's okay, Bub. It was a way back. Things are different nowadays to what they were then," Joe conceded.

"I don't feel I am honourable enough to continue working on the film, Joe. I feel my presence has sullied it or something now I know," I continued, almost crying.

"Sure you are, your noonaa brolga - champion woman, Gwabadag Gaany - beautiful spirit. We have to keep going with this sister. It is time for us all to move forward into healing. This is our job to do," Joe explained as I wiped away the warm, salty streams silently trickling down my face.

So, we finished the movie, "Displaced Voices[9]" and it didn't get as much publicity or reach as many people as we thought it might. Perhaps for political reasons or maybe because of my editing prowess or lack of. We'd given it our best shot with all the resources available.

We invested all of our focus, our time and energy on this project for over three months and developed a very close brother/sister type relationship. Once we birthed the project, we had to let it go. Joe is definitely one man I would call upon if I ever needed help, and I know that he would always have my back. It was yet another practice of Ishvara Pranidhana, and through that emerges the much bigger story of forgiveness, deep love, and healing.

We have done a lot of work together in the years following.

---

9. Link to the movie: https://youtu.be/u2xBhSyx5IM

Photoshoots, editing and publishing books, driven to Uluru and back together for Joe to attend a historical conference on the referendum vote. This was where the important political statement was released from the Aboriginal people to the Government - 'Uluru Statement of the Heart'. Through our involvement, I have also taught yoga and meditation to Aboriginal youth.

At the beginning of the year in Australia, a particular day is marked for a public holiday to celebrate the introduction of white settlement, 'Australia Day'. Typically, it's a day where people overindulge in drinking beer and throw sausages and seafood on the BBQ. It's a day I find cringeworthy, though I'll admit that wasn't always the case. Naturally, this is a difficult day for those who are non-Caucasians, akin to dancing upon their graves and their loss, 'Invasion Day.' I usually do a Pro-Aboriginal post; however this year was encouraged by Spirt to enlist assistance. Soul brother's Joe, Julian Silburn and Scott Chisholm (ex-Australian Football League Player) and Christine and son, Tim Morrison, his partner Sammi Davies joined me to bring forth a renamed "Day of Healing Ceremony."

We held it at the beach as the sun set, and opened it to everyone, kids included. Over a hundred people came. We shared some culture with ochre-covered faces and stories. There was a smoking ceremony and an opportunity to learn some aboriginal dance with the young men who were there. Scott and Joe talked about the truth of their experiences within the society we all live in. Which was like taking the lid off to drink from a whole new bottle for most. On top of this, there was a healing circle where we could Gift our intention for the future into the middle. It was a powerful ceremony, and the Elders and Ancestors supported us with our work that day. You could feel it in the 'god bumps.'

As the sunset's magnificent magnolia bloom dropped out of view beyond the shoreline, spreading her orange halo for infinite miles, we stood together. Mums, Dads, Neighbours, Brothers, Sisters, Sons, Daughters, Cousins, Black, White, United, as One people, casting our Sankalpa (intention) across the waters, past the Wagyl, all the way out to Dreamtime in the Cosmos. In the space of our Heart. Our Awakening

Spiritual Heart's. We created a Universal Consciousness. It became a large thought-form which evoked a more significant impact than merely one person. It felt like something magical happened that day.

In the literal writing of this part of the book, Ken Wyatt, a First Nations man, was inducted as the first ever Minister for Indigenous Affairs in Parliament. A long time coming, though, a step in the right direction for the First Nations People of Australia. The next step would be to offer the Aboriginal people the 'right' to able to vote for the best candidate for this position. I'm reminded of Gregg Braden's work[10], which encourages us to remember we can alter the outcomes of future events by Prayer in groups. Did our work on the day do this? No way of knowing. Truth is just 'do the work as they instruct you to' and then practice 'Ishvara pranidhana' letting it all go. Surrender. We don't need all the answers, we just have to trust.

---

10. The Isiah Effect: Decoding the Lost Science of Prayer

Chapter Twelve

THROUGH MOVEMENT
I CONNECT AND GROUND

Asana

Playlist – Stevie Wonder - Higher Ground 1973

In Patanjali's ancient wisdom of yoga the correct series of events is that we make our way through the five Yamas - the things not to do. The five Niyamas - the things we are to do through the outer observances and the inner observances and then we make our way to asana, the movement part of yoga. Interestingly, in the fifty-one sutras, and the one hundred and ninety-six aphorisms, he only mentioned the word 'asana' three times. Yet this forms the solid foundation and almost the entirety of most western 'yoga' classes, and what many believe 'yoga' to be about. Physical movement of the body.

The 'asana' Patanjali refers to is the ability to sit in a seated posture that is steady, stable and comfortable. With little tension or effort, one is free from suffering and able to do the meditation practices that create allowance to gain mastery of thought patterns of the mind field, ultimately merging with the infinite. (http://www.swamij.com/yoga-sutras-24648.htm) Then we are no longer upset by the play of opposites.

In translating Sanskrit, the word 'asana' means 'a comfortable seat.' Yet, when most of us say, we are heading out to a yoga class, for the bulk of us this means we will do asana - the physical practice of yoga. And it would upset many if the only pose they did all class were just 'sitting in a comfortable seat'. In modern times, in the West, the third limb of Patanjali's sutras, and the word 'asana' is utilised to describe the practice of physical movement of the body through postures. Which is what we commonly call 'doing yoga.' In its very most straightforward form 'hatha' yoga. Yoga of the sun 'ha' and the moon 'tha' bringing our masculine and feminine qualities, the outer and the inner, below and above, back and front into balance.

I saw a Vedic astrologer, Dr Theja from the Australian Institute of Vedic Astrology and he did my chart for me, back in 2011.

"Oh dear, you have so much Mars energy, it is so important for you to ground this energy; otherwise you will be all over the place," he said. "For some people I say, yoga (asana) might be good. For you, it is a daily requirement. Otherwise, you go flying off all over the place."

This was funny for me to hear, being about eighteen months into my dedicated daily practice. I agreed with him. Daily practice of yoga asana suited me. I'd seen the benefits already.

Without a doubt, the practice of asana as modern yoga decree's, (the postures) have been and continue to be my Saving Grace. It has been the sacred altar I have repeatedly knelt and prayed at, throughout the course of my life. This is the key that unlocks the door to higher Self - Mastery for me. It is what brings me back to the essence of 'who I am' and allows an aspiration to be a much better version. To strive to be Greater, to burn brightly. The physical practice of asana has taught me so much in the past and continues to be my most excellent teacher. Mastery through movement was a pathway I was blessed to have opened up for me at an early age, through gymnastics and yoga. Daily, it offers me the opportunity to take my gaze inwards. To be the observer of my 'self'. To honour my breath, to witness the movement of energy in my body. It's the space to consider where I feel blocked or restrained and to ponder how this is outplaying in my external world. To perceive where I am fluid and flexible. It is a reminder to have fun, to be open to exploration and experimentation in ways that honour and respect the 'vehicle' I have been gifted to journey with.

My daily asana offers the 'playground' to practice the first two limbs of yoga, the Yama's and the Niyama's on the mat. To reinforce and remind me of their meaning. To ensure I practice with loving kindness and compassion (ahimsa). I listen to the truth (satya) of my body's messages in the present moment, practicing contentment (santosha), challenging myself without pushing too far and injuring myself (aparigraha). Otherwise I understand I am 'stealing' from myself (asteya) in that 'dishonour'. My commitment to remain alcohol-free, my ten-year experiment, a longitudinal study in brahmacharya, (abstinence) and saucha (purity) also provided in the 'refinement of moderation' in my physical asanas. Plus a training ground in self-discipline, and a honing of what to feed the senses (tapas). In structured simplicity, each yoga posture provides an opportunity to study and witness the landscape of my body, the topography of my mind (svadhyaya). And to find the gateway to the Divine, upon where I surrender (ishvara pranidhana) and let it all go.

My path has been an errant one. It has been a long and winding road, through different experiences. I've had numerous teachers and tried many styles of yoga asana. I have traversed on my mat through Hatha the umbrella of all yoga styles, Ashtanga, Vinyasa, Iyengar, Forrest, Bikram, Restorative and Yin. Some of my favourite teachers to practice with and learn from are Mark Whitwell, Ana Forrest, Shiva Rea and Kali Ma Shub in Perth. I am deeply inspired by Krishnamacharya's teachings, the granddaddy of all modern-day yoga. Long-time student, Mark Whitwell jokes that Krishnamacharya was the original 'insta-famous' yogi. He had himself photographed way back in the day. He was the teacher to Lyengar and

Pattabhi Jois who developed their own definitive and very different styles, which have become known worldwide.

Mostly, Krishnamacharya's teachings encourage that yoga is for 'everybody' and this approach appeals to me in my private practice and in the way I teach. I appreciate and have embodied personally that at different stages of our lives, depending upon what we have going on, we need assorted styles of yoga. I know while I coped with my mum dying I practiced the very 'hardcore' yang and physically demanding, type A personality, styles of yoga Bikram and Ashtanga. These enabled me to deal with a lack of control over my external experience and regain my perceived locus of control, through repetitive practices of *sequences that remain the same*. Consequently, maintaining a *sense* of control - a little like madly bailing water out of a sinking ship. The moment my beautiful mum died, literally, I stopped practicing such extreme forms, and became more loving, and kind in my approach to my asana practice. I needed love, and that was what I honoured myself with. This all occurred innately, body-led, rather than something I consciously chose.

A gentler, more compassionate style of asana is in most cases, precisely what we all need, though not something that we will often gift ourselves. Most of us see our yoga practice is our physical workout. That it needs to be 'burning' a particular amount of calories, enabling us to lose weight or shape the body in some specific way. I have heard Pattabhi Jois created Ashtanga yoga for fourteen-year-old boys, which makes little sense for the amount of western men and women over forty practicing it. Our bodies have different needs at different stages of our lives. Though, *as long as one is truly listening to their bodies own truth, and they practice the asana with loving kindness,* then it doesn't matter what particular style it is being practiced. A *practice* is a practice. Often, people come to yoga with the same approach to other forms of exercise, to 'beat the body into submission'. Yoga asana practice reveres one's body, it is *praying at the temple*, offering flowers to the *sacred home of our spirit*, not the desecration. In truth, an asana sadhana is a daily opportunity *to connect into all that truly is*, which is on the **inside**, not the **outside**. Though they can often reflect one another, the micro **is** the macro.

You can attend all the classes you want, and it's great to have group experiences, but it is my belief gained through my practical experience over the years, that all the magic happens in creating and committing to daily practice at home. Setting up your own space, making it sacred, and connecting with this place daily is where you will find yourself and allow your own truth to unfold. Sure, it's great and beneficial to connect in with teachers, however often you need, though not at the expense of **your own** sadhana. In the current world platform, where so many gurus (teachers) are being bought down by misuse of power, the best Guru you can commit to, is yourself. An Eckhart Tolle quote explains:

"For most people, their spiritual teacher is their suffering. Because eventually, the suffering brings about awakening."

And we can tune into that by creating the space within our lives to do so, creating the pause between the inhalation and the exhalation, to really tune into where we are at. My dearly loved Nanna Violet, Aboriginal Elder with whom I am incredibly blessed to spend a lot of time and teachings with says to me that yoga is actually an acronym. It stands for '**Y**our **O**wn **G**od **A**wareness' and I like this. It is the connection and the pathway to the Divine.

***

One of the best things I did after the momentous wake-up call at age forty was the implementation of my ten-year experiment. This gifted me the impetus to execute a life of refinement and more enormous growth, and part of this was to create a unique dedicated space to practice in. I didn't even have a mat for the first couple of years. I had my white buddha, some crystals, some sweets, and flowers, and my mala[11] beads on a wooden ledge that became my altar. I made a commitment to myself I would get up **every** morning at 5am and practice asana and meditation in my special place of worship, for at **least** an hour every day. It served me and continues to in so many ways. Sure, there have been days where I found it

---

11. beads like rosary typically made from neem or sandalwood in India, to purchase: http://mandijnelson.com/index.php/product-category/products

difficult when it was freezing cold, and the thought of getting up was way more complicated than the reality. And still others I've just sat on the mat because I wasn't feeling well.

On the whole, I've shown up for myself daily. This sadhana keeps me vital, my body supple and flexible, robust, healthy, and lean. It encourages me to get to bed earlier, influences the food I eat, has allowed me to continue my path of purification. That which no longer serves me falling away with little actual effort required from the personality of 'me'. I said 'yes' to a daily practice and then opened my ears to listen to the messages of my heart. I created the space literally and figuratively to observe and witness my 'self', through asana, which naturally and organically, extended beyond the physical practice. My practice nowadays fluctuates from between twenty minutes to a couple of hours, daily.

Through my physical sadhana, I opened the Golden Gateway and crossed the bridge to my heart. I have lived this way as a permanent fixture, rather than just merely 'band-aiding' my latest drama as I did previously, for almost the past ten years. My life has been such a beautiful co-creation within the natural flow of life. My heart, intuition and inspiration always deliver me where I 'need' to go, working with the Divine. I must drop my ego, and hand over the 'controls' to something higher than me. I could not have written the story of the last decade better for myself if I tried. It has been such an incredibly magical, unfolding journey.

My favourite practices follow the 'believed to be' absolute roots of where yoga (asana) practice first began. The honouring of the sun and the moon through prayer and movement. This is what 'ha' 'tha' yoga represents, the union of the sun (masculine) aspects of ourselves, with the lunar (feminine) aspects of ourselves for the ultimate union. Yoga means 'to yoke' - to bind - to create union. More profound yogic philosophy speaks of the union of the 'Ida' (feminine - lunar aspects) and the 'Pingala' (masculine - solar aspects) through the Sushumna - kundalini energy. This runs up the spine, with both facets meeting at each of the Nadi - chakra points of the body. So, I seek to create a union within my physical body through the Divine Masculine and Divine Feminine as reflected through my sadhana. My practice through salutations to the sun, 'Surya Namaskar[12]' with chanting - which form the ancient tantric roots of yoga, and through the honouring of the moon 'Chandra Namaskar[13]' allow a union within my 'being' and an affinity and connectedness with the external natural environment. It has helped me to cultivate an honouring of my own physical body as a **vessel** and the 'Great Mother', as the **vessel** upon which I live and am sustained upon and by. I connect and create union within and a union without, with the elements, the seasons and nature, all that is. Again, the micro reflects the macro. I have gained greater respect and place a much higher worth upon the human body and this incredible planetary body we have the privilege to walk upon, with love and beauty. In coming to find self-honour and love, I have also found **love** and **honour** of all things. The inner reflects the outer.

The practice of yoga asana also assists us to move and shift energy within and around the body. We refer to this as 'prana' or vital life force. We utilise the breath, yogic postures and our intent - Sankalpa - to cleanse and clear blockages. The physical body is the densest expression of our 'selves,' and everything we experience passes through it. This means unless we are actively cleansing and clearing the physical body with intent through an asana practice that energy will become blocked, sometimes creating 'dis-ease' or distress. I also like to play or chant mantra while I practice, or in classes I teach. I often enlist the assistance of experienced and accomplished live musicians and sound healers within the field as nada (sound) yoga, such as Julian Silburn, Christine Morrison, Kim Ecchamaal, and John Whife. This takes the benefits of the practice to another 'level' as it is a multi-disciplined approach with more healing and higher clearing capacity. And it adds to create a spectacular group experience.

There is some debate and little respect from those who teach more traditional styles of yoga encompassing the 'old teachings' for those straight 'asana' physical-based classes. The straight 'asana' classes I refer to offer little or no philosophy, thereby present no opportunity for the 'tip

---

12. link to Surya Namaskar with chanting https://youtu.be/bdJQi-i8xkY
13. link to Chandra Namaskar https://youtu.be/CW19gIJ4AFg

of the iceberg' to be explored further, or so it would seem. I would argue it takes different styles of yoga for different people. Eventually, no matter what style you practice - even asana only, you're still drinking from the font. The water from the well will infiltrate the cellular body, changing, enabling transmutation and transformation, one drop at a time. It might take a little longer to get there, however inevitably through the physical practice itself, a change in consciousness will transpire. You will open up like the majestic lotus flower. Maybe completely this lifetime, maybe the next. All in good time. There are many paths up the mountain. And there is not *one* that is suitable for everyone. We each must find our own way. Some will create their own, and others will jump on the highway that everyone else is taking.

* * *

The physical practice of yoga for me is as comfortable as putting on a pair of worn-in slippers. There is Ease and Grace. When I am in Rishikesh, India, I feel such an affinity with the Sadhus and swamis, I feel like I have come home. For me now, the practice of asana and meditation, and working my way continually through the Yama's and Niyamas is a 'no-brainer'. It feels like it always existed within my cells, dormant until I opened the space in my life for it to re-awaken. When I am amongst those who have taken steps to walk this path, I feel I am in my natural environment. I experience Santosha and Ananda (bliss).

There is a western yogini, a teacher, Tao Percheron, who is 100 (in 2019) and still teaching yoga. When I grow up, I want to be just like her.

Chapter Thirteen

BREATHE WITH ME

Pranayama

Playlist – Fleurie – Breathe 2016

At my most dramatic, and extremely unwell, I smoked two packets of cigarettes a day. This didn't allow much space for a natural, spontaneous breath. My breath was short and sharp, with occasional 'biting' pains in my chest. In fact, there was hardly a breath that didn't involve inhaling the toxic chemicals of tailor-made cigarettes within my waking hours. It was almost impossible to take a deep breath, to fully inhale, and thus to invite 'life' in. My life force was low, my etheric field contaminated and my willingness to live negligible. It is often said that smoking is a slow suicide, and now I'm on the other side of it, I have to agree. I stubbornly maintained my on again off again relationship to cigarettes for many years, almost twenty-seven to be exact, even sacrilegiously smoking through my pregnancies. At least I cut down to a minimal five a day then. And whilst

I was very good at quitting, I was equally good at taking the habit back up again. It served me to some degree, just don't question me exactly how, and I fed myself the belief it was only 'hurting me' if I believed it was. I was under the notion we are our thoughts, and what we think we bring into manifestation.

I continued to smoke for a further two years. Even while I crafted and cultivated my commitment to a daily practice of yoga and embarked upon my ten-year experiment of 'alcohol - free,' actively pursuing the path of 'being the best version of me'. Finally, I quit. Then, a year later, before Mum's passing, I broke my foot in a couple of places after coming off a scooter in Bali. Since I couldn't practice asana, I took up smoking again, sneaking outside the front of the house so my kids didn't find out. They caught me. It was pretty embarrassing. I puffed on cigarettes for three months while my bones in my foot healed until I could resume my physical practice. Please don't try this at home, smoking is not conducive to healing bones. That was my last dance though, and since then I have not returned. I don't crave cigarettes, the part of me just simply is not there anymore.

***

The fourth limb of yoga, according to Patanjali's ancient wisdom, is Pranayama. We can break down the Sanskrit translation of the word as follows. 'Prana' is breath, respiration, vital or visog, spirit. Prana enlivens everything within the universe, it's the life force also described as subtle energy we can access indirectly through the breath. The meaning of 'Ayama' is control, or restraint and expansion and stretching. Thus, Pranayama is commonly known as either 'breath control," breath expansion' or 'expansion of life force.' Many also speak to its capacity at an advanced level of use.

It allows, "Access to the great universal force/awakening, known as Mahan Prāṇā. As an advanced practice, Prāṇāyāma guides our individual prāṇā into alignment with this universal force/awakening. Such alignment helps us experience our highest self in union with universal consciousness. As we pass through the layers of the body and the mind, we are brought into relationship with this force/awakening, so we can realise our fullest potential." Jenny Hayo https://8limbsyoga.com/pranayama-the-4th-limb-of-yoga/

The simplest form of pranayama is to simply observe your breath. To slow your life down enough to witness the one thing that happens spontaneously without effort yet maintains and underwrites our journey here upon the planet. The inhalation and the exhalation. Interestingly, according to 'Heart of Yoga' by Deskichar, though this practice seems an easy one, it was only taught to the highest, most dedicated of yogic practitioners. For me, as I first began to witness my breath, I noticed my breathing became all 'shy'. It started to move within me erratically as I felt I ought to breathe in some particular manner. The breath and the observation of it is such an excellent barometer of how our practice, and life, is tracking.

Sometimes we find we are breathing heavily on our mat, our breath is shallow, or we are finding it challenging to maintain a comfortable, steady pace. This is often an indicator we are pushing things too hard, a sign to back up a little. Ideally, we want our breath to remain as our natural, spontaneous breath throughout the physical yoga practice, unless we are practicing specific pranayama. Those that build heat 'kababhati' - breath of fire (breath creating forceful exhalations) or 'ujai'[14] (throat breathing, blending inhalation with expansion of the diaphragm and exhalation draws abdominals in towards the spine.) This also increases oxygenation and helps to maintain rhythm, taking the practice to a Zen level.

A practice of pranayama I love to share with my students is 'vilomna', which means breathing against the natural rhythm of your breath. It is particularly beneficial to turn on the parasympathetic nervous system, thus switching off the flight/fight response. It works on the premise that when we are stressed or anxious; we lose control of our breath, which becomes erratic. Vilomna[15] brings us back to our natural state of breath by breathing first against that natural state. It is such a handy tool to carry

---

14. link to ujai breathing practice https://youtu.be/BNjuW_MC9hU
15. link to vilomna breathing practice https://youtu.be/KdIA_Y5q0uc

in your back pocket, particularly if you suffer from stress or anxiety. It also offers the following benefits:

- Calm the body and mind
- Reduce anxiety and tension
- Relax the nervous system
- Boost lung capacity
- Energise and cool the body

Please use the link to a free download for you to practice or to pass onto others that might need it. Similarly, a simple way of quickly reinforcing a state of more ease with the breath is to make the exhalation longer than the inhalation. You can work with this easily, perhaps making the inhalation to the count of four and the exhalation to the count of six, or whatever variable best suits your lung capacity.

BKS Iyengar, one of the yoga greats, stated, "If you control your breath, you control your mind."

When the breath is unsteady, so is the mind. I have heard many a teacher state the quality of our breath controls the quality of our life. What quality of life are you choosing?

***

The night before my mum passed, I inherently knew to stay the night at my parents' house, even though where I lived was less than five minutes' drive away. We were caring for my mum in their home, with the Silver Chain Organisation in intermittent attendance. Despite her oncologist indicating she could have two weeks to live and given the fact we were only four days into that, her death still felt imminent. I received a clear message by my intuition, heart or from 'source' to stay. Four years into my ten-year experiment, I was that 'connected' and 'tuned' into listening and trusting my own inner voice or directly dialling up 'Spirit' I knew to take heed. For four years, I had solely trusted that 'voice' and it had not led me astray.

It is said that once you take away a person's pain, death will come soon. For years my mum survived bone cancer with barely any pain relief, at her own choosing. The doctors regularly gave her scripts, but she refused to take more than Panadol. At the end of her life, she must have been in incredible pain for the amount of morphine proscribed. When we began administrating the medicine as instructed and diagnosed by her doctor, this would have immediately taken away her suffering. On the morning she died; the night proceeding had been the first in twenty years all four of her children had stayed together under the same roof in the family home.

I slept close to my parents' room, where my mum's respite was set up, in the lounge room. I awakened for the second time at about six forty-five that morning. The first time when I had spontaneously woken at three am, my dad assured me he would get me if I 'needed' to be there. The second time I awakened with a 'start' jumping out of bed to check on my mum. I entered their room with trepidation. Instinctively I felt she didn't have much longer here upon the planet. Though the bed she lay in was only a single bed, with my dad's empty one next to it, her frail body seemed to take up the entire room. I checked her breathing and knew her time was almost complete. Her breath was faint, and it felt as though she was drifting from us. I heard her inhale, softly, big pause, then gently exhale. I placed my hand gently on her head, stroking her hair.

We'd been doing some death meditations in the days leading up to this point to help her passage through.

My youngest sister, Kate, was also awakened and came into the room. I indicated to her she didn't have long with my look. She sat on the other side of the bed to me.

We heard her inhale, softly, a big pause, then gently exhale.

"It's okay, Mum. You can go to the Light. We love you so much and thank you for all you have done. We release you now," I said softly.

We heard her inhale, softly, a big pause, then gently exhale.

"Go to the Light, Mum. We love you soooo much," said Kate, who had always had an exceptional connection with our mum.

We heard her inhale, softly, a big pause, then gently exhale.

My dad came in at this point. I'm not sure where he'd been.

"Dad, it's time," I gently said. He looked lost. And a little confused.

We heard her inhale, softly, a big pause, then gently exhale.

"You'd better get Melanie and Garth."

Kate and I sat with my mum, listening and holding onto her breath while my dad went to get my brother and sister.

We heard her inhale, softly, a big pause, then gently exhale.

Time wavered like blurring vision on a rainy windscreen, like the travelling longitude waves of frequency in vibration. They are seen and heard but impeccable and indescribably intangible. My mum's lifeline and connection to us were fading, and time was warping. I was energetically focussing on love, sending her all the love I could muster. Not an attachment style of love, a universal form of love, of non-attachment, of joy and bliss, emanating out of my heart space, hopefully making its way to hers.

My other sister, Melanie, came into the room, and sat at the end of the bed.

We heard my mum inhale, softly, a big pause, then gently exhale.

"Mum, go to the Light. We love you," she said with a sob.

My dad came back in to the room.

"Where's Garth?" I whispered.

We heard her inhale, softly, a more significant pause, then gently exhale.

"He's coming," said my dad in a low voice.

He'd better hurry, I thought.

My mum inhaled, long, slowly, softly and just as she did, my brother walked through the door, then she exhaled.

And we waited for the next inhalation, but that was it.

There was no more breath. Her spirit had left her human body.

Just as my brother walked in the door, majestically, she gifted us the greatest, most beautiful gift of all. The gift of our own life and the gift of sharing her death. All of us. Not one or the other but all of us who she loved, that her Love had Created.

And never before this was I acutely aware of the **infinite** power of the breath.

Through this most sacred experience, I found the honour and privilege, the lesson of the one thing, the most important thing, that keeps us rooted in our journey here upon this planet, our Breath.

Such a perfect, divine, and infinite Gift from my mother, given in so many powerful ways throughout our lives together as she deepened my inherent understanding of the untold unilateral supremacy of the breath.

Until that point it had probably been lip-service. After this life-altering, life deepening most reverent and berated of all experiences upon this planet, I offered my blessings and wholeheartedly, somewhat belatedly bowed at the feet of my mother. I opened my heart to love the Great Mother, our planet, and the Cosmic Mother. This last infinite offering from my mother to me was the Gateway to comprehending the greatest most obvious secrets to life itself, the absolutely **immense** capacity of our **breath**.

>Consequently, forever changing how I approach pranayama.
>With honour, sacredness, intent, reverence, and devotion.
>
>Om purnamadah purnamidam purnat purnamudachyate,
>purnasya purnamadaya purnameva avashishyate.
>Om Shantih Shantih Shantih.

That is complete, this complete. From the complete, the complete is taken, the complete has come. If you take the complete from the complete, the complete alone remains.
Om Peace, Peace, Peace.

Chapter Fourteen

SENSELESS

Pratyahara

Playlist – Maggie Clifford, Mooji Mala, Omkara - Amazing Grace 2017

At eighteen, my senses or 'indriyas' drove me. I'd moved out of home and lived in a share house near the coast. Dependent upon whose girlfriends stayed the night, there could be between four to seven other people there. The core 'housemates' were four guys. I lived in the garage with my boyfriend. A typical day would begin with heaving up the garage door, making my way to the inside toilet, having a couple of brekkie 'cones' - some marijuana. Then we'd head back to bed to make love.

A few hours later, my boyfriend and I would go into the main house to find a feed of something - usually greasy and fattening, bacon, sausages, egg, baked beans. It depended on where we were placed in relation to 'shopping' day and assuming no one else had already eaten our supplies from the shared fridge. From here, we would check the swell and most days in the summer we'd drive down to the local beach for a couple of hours.

While the boys surfed, I would catch up with the girls for some inane gossip, lying g-string-clad, lizard-like in the sun. We'd flick through the latest 'Dolly' or "Cosmopolitan' magazines, intermittently drooling over either some new piece of clothing, makeup or some beautiful male specimen as he walked past carrying his board. After a couple of hours passed, we would go back to the guys' house to make love again and fill our stomachs once more. Then the 'goon bag' (wine cask) and bucket would get pulled out for an afternoon's 'entertainment' and priming for the evening. Sculls and 'bucket bongs', crazed games, and dares, all intending to make sure one of the male 'core' housemates got more 'wasted' than the rest. The 'victim' would invariably be made fun of in their inebriated state. There'd be eyebrows shaved, and moustached or phallic symbols marked on their face in black permanent marker as they lay senseless and passed out upon the floor. Then the rest of us would leave to go 'party' some more at a local bar or nightclub in the city. Perhaps 'dropping' an LSD trip or tab of 'E.' It was a hedonistic lifestyle. One that Freud would have referred to as being driven by the 'Id' - or the pleasure principle, driven by the senses.

My senses and pursuing pleasure drove most of my behaviour for many years. I was 'blessed' to be born in Western society, in a middle-class family. I didn't have any familial responsibilities. Well, none I wished to adopt anyhow. I was illuminated by such conduct of ruthlessly chasing the next hit when I was using drugs or laying stoned from heroin inert, unable to move from the floor. By staying up all night having taken amphetamines or ecstasy, 'cutting up' a dance floor, followed by hours and hours of copulation where no one could reach climax because of the drug. Through to spending idle hours in shopping centres, buying the 'perfect' dress, or having my hair or nails done. In my one-sided lack of self- restraint, ultimately, from time to time, the pendulum would swing the other way, and I would experience the dual end of the stick - suffering.

As a youngster, I scarred myself falling over drunk. I ended up vomiting, passing out and sleeping in a bush. I was taken advantage of and sexually assaulted on numerous occasions because my sense-driven behaviour had rendered me 'senseless.' 'The lights are on but no one's home' type of scenario. Many a night I'd wake up with that sinking feeling in the pit of my stomach with no idea what transpired the night before. I could remember up to a certain point and then… blackout.

Friends died from drug overdoses and HIV. I lost others to arrest, police run-ins and the riot squad. It took me a long time to learn self-control and self-moderation. To make the connection between annihilation and suffering. To understand the consequences of overindulgence and adversity and anguish. Or to find the courage to move beyond the behaviour of my peers, and to gain some understanding about the laws of Karma and spiritual growth.

There is a moral tale about the feather, the brick, and the truck. It is said that Spirit will send us messages to assist us in our path. To help us choose the right course of action. Initially, those messages will be gentle, like the stroke of a feather, though if we pay no heed, they will 'up the ante' to throwing a figurative brick at us. And if we still do not heed the signs, Spirit will drive a Mac truck straight at us. Spirit inherently wants us to grow and learn, it's the essence of our journey here.

So, concerning my pleasure-seeking behaviour, Spirit initially sent me little messages about adverse effects from my behaviour, like perhaps feeling dizzy, or unwell from overindulgence. (Feather - I'm getting the message that too much alcohol isn't working for me.) Then if I paid no attention, I might end up in the toilet, vomiting and pass out there, waking to a puke-covered dress created from a technicolour yawn. (Brick - a more severe message about the unsuitability of my chosen use of alcohol. It's embarrassing walking through a bar with vomit all over you. It doesn't matter how hard you try, even if you get the puke out of your clothing, you cannot get rid of the smell). Finally, if I still paid no attention, I might crash my uninsured car through driving under the influence and then get done for drink driving. (And this is the truck - the unmistakable message that things need to change. Things have hit the wall).

And all the stories are true. Thankfully, as my practice and dedication deepened, and as I grew older and somewhat wiser, I started to listen to Spirit and my essential truth or Source. I withdrew my focus from merely acting from upon unconscious behaviour of flattering the indriyas (senses).

***

A yogic practice and Patanjali's Fifth Limb encourage the practitioner to move into states of pure consciousness, the deep well of the True Self. This can only be accessed by 'controlling our senses.' I know this as 'Pratyahara.' It refers to 'moving our awareness' from our five senses, including the information we receive externally and internally. It means more than sitting down and closing our eyes because even in this state, our mind can be 'revisiting' sensory information. We can be 'thinking' about the knowledge we have gleaned through the senses. It is the capacity to be the observer of our sensory information, without acting unconsciously according to what we perceive. It is to remove the 'reactionary self' from the equation and though this practice to be better responders and thus 'response-able' - responsible.

So, as an example, I might feel the urge for chocolate and wait to see what happens, if I don't feed this 'need.' You can explore this for yourself with anything you consciously or subconsciously use to 'escape' your present reality. It could be sex, alcohol, or other drugs, food, sugar, shopping, monetary gain, any of the 'seven deadly sins.' When we practice Pratyahara, it's not submerging or withdrawing from those needs but to witness them. So, to stop using drugs many years ago, I needed to first be able to 'see' my thoughts. To quieten down my 'ahamkara' -the ego, and the thinking part (mana) and allow the Buddhi space to purely observe.

Society, and I speak to Western culture because that is where I live, mostly, wants us to remain unconscious. Bouncing from one sensory need to the next. For while we are externally focussed we are easy to control. While we continue to be concerned about how we look, what we wear, the car we drive, and the 'right' suburbs to live in, we are forced to make more money. This ensures we remain plugged into the larger matrix. And we stay living in the realms of superficiality, blindly adopting beliefs and norms without question as though they were our own. Conversely, pure consciousness, which is the aim of yogic practice of Pratyahara, cannot be smelled, tasted, seen, touched or heard, it exists beyond these. So, in quiet pursuit of Pratyahara, we move intentionally inwards to explore something more magnificent than which we can find externally. It is the pathway we must seek to gain control of our senses to gain self-mastery or self-realisation. Many texts speak of the senses being like the worker bees and the mind, the Queen Bee. So, if the Queen Bee focuses on pursuing and pleasuring the senses, the worker bees will create this as our reality. If we focus the Queen Bee mind inward, the worker bees will focus inward. The question is, how do we get that to happen?

It took a lot of internal will power, which we know as Tapas, courage and a deep desire for constitutional change for me to decide. I then had to direct my Queen Bee, and as a by-product, worker bees, to walk the path of a yogi. To adopt a practice of Saucha (cleanliness) and Brahmacharya (abstinence) in committing to a yogic practice daily. In a society such as Australia that thrives on the whole, 'crack a beer, eat a meat pie as you watch the footy' culture, it meant I needed to make a firm stand against my senses. And abstain from the customs of my nation and peer group to make decisions in line with my highest growth. The key to this decision was the suffering at the hand of living indulgently driven by my senses was no longer viable for me. I'd made a clear, firm decision about *what I didn't want to* continue to create. This lead to my ten-year experiment, committed daily practice of yoga, and untold personal growth.

Once we move the focus inwards, this is where we experience the 'deep well' of nothingness from which all is created. We know it via quantum physics as the zero point field. It is the field of blackness, not unlike what I experienced after hitting death all those many years ago. Where we feel all and nothing simultaneously. We allow our personality 'selves' that offer us the body to experience through our senses, yet concurrently keep us separate from it all. We surrender and allow our 'selves' to drop into the infinite ocean of All That Is, and All That Was. In this similar space to that which we all originally birthed from, our mothers' womb. From out of this cavernous well, we find deep listening. From this fathomless listening, we hear the voice of our own inherent, essential truth. Some might say this is how we access more clearly our Divine spark. It is how it worked for me. This is the profound reservoir the practice of Pratyahara offers us as it forms the bridge between our inner and outer worlds. Furthermore, it becomes the gateway between the external limbs we have already discussed. The Yama's, Niyamas, Asana and Pranayama, opening the Golden Pathway to the internal and final limbs in the complete practice, deepening our understanding and connection to our own God Awareness.

Chapter Fifteen

SINGLE POINT OF FOCUS

Dharana

Playlist - Bob Marley and the Wailers - One Love/People Get Ready 1965

From the bridge of the practice of Pratyahara evolves the pathway to the remaining three limbs in the embodiment in the Eightfold journey of yoga, according to the ancient text of Patanjali's sutras. These all relate to stages of concentration. Swamiji refers to these as below.

Stages of attention: It is attention itself, which is progressively moving inward through these few stages:

- Attention leads to concentration (dharana). (3.1)
- Concentration leads to meditation (dhyana). (3.2)
- Meditation leads to absorption (samadhi). (3.3)

"Describe your most beautiful moment," I ask as I am sitting, with ears-pricked and primed, professional ear-muff audio earphones on, hands gripped around the DSLR upon the tripod. I keep a check on the focus of the camera I am closest to and the one I have set up across the room, for the alternative angle. I am filming in the house of Jason River, whom I met a little under an hour ago. "This process - the CherishYOU process, is a gift for him from a group of friends for his fiftieth birthday. Jason is dying of metastasized prostate cancer, and he has two young children and a loving, devoted wife. This process is to memorialise him. To bind his memories, thoughts, and his essence to film. To allow him to reflect upon his life and tell his story so it is heard in his words. So his wife, Wendy, and his children have something tangible to anchor them as the need arises when his physical presence has passed. I have a single point of focus. My concentration is razor-sharp as I endeavour to produce an exquisite, unique, poignant gift for the family. I bind my consciousness to a single spot. At this moment, my focus is with diamond-like precision to capture the best quality footage and sound within my capacity. My senses high, tuned to anything that might distract or muddy the calibre, and *genuinely being present to what Jason is sharing*. I have to '*feel*' my way through this to honour his process and utilise my mind and knowledge in a technological, technical sense. In the next moment, I will anchor my mind to the 'following question' I will ask him. Tomorrow I will direct my concentration to the production side of this invaluable project.

The editing of my voice out of the footage. The addition of photographs and music he has shared with me that are his favourite. The analysis of which piece of footage is best to use from which angle and the marriage of this with the external sound recording I've captured is our creation. Traditional constructs of 'time' will slip away from me as I work to produce the highest quality, the best effort I can achieve with this sacred offering of honouring and cherishing Jason's life. I will sometimes work all night, will forget to drink and eat, and be consumed by the birthing of this project until I complete it.

This practical application of Dharana grew out of a 'heart whispering'.

A listening to my internal voice to film my grandparents before they passed. As my dedication to my yogic path deepened, my understanding and embodiment of the sutras of Patanjali expanded by proxy, really, I didn't have to try at this. I firmly committed to listening to that 'heart whispering,' that spark of the Divine that spoke to me and acting upon that always. I realised the *CherishYOU* process was a gift of reciprocity. Something of immense value I could offer others, that gave *infinitely*, an invaluable provision to humanity much needed. Just as 'Pratyahara' dictates, if we fine-tune our mind, we can also fine-tune our senses to be working 'for' and not against the mind. And Pratyahara leads to a gateway belying the boddhi mind, to the universal consciousness.

In direct proportion, the deeper my yogic sadhana, the *more profound my experience of life*. The longer that I dedicated upon this path, the more I was offered. To begin with, my focus might have been more asana based. As time went on, by continually 'drinking at the well,' and reading voraciously within the field, a vaster concept of reality opened for me than I thought possible. Beyond the trappings of superficiality my younger life was consumed by, mindlessly following the direction of my 'senses', experiential escapism, my practice led me to explore realms of existence I thought to be mere illusionary. Concepts I paid 'lip service' to became part of my conscious awareness, part of my direct experience. Spirit has an incredible way of creating the most fantastic weave when we are open to listening. And what we focus upon is what we create. Gandhi said, "Be the change you wish to see in the world" for the simple reason if we make the change internally, we will affect change externally too. Take the focus inwards. Affect the difference there. And watch it ripple out.

I was aware from my asana practice, and thus what I taught, of the left side of the body is the feminine. The right considered the masculine, the left the 'moon' and the right the 'sun'. And that asana aims to embody internal unification between the two. It is the internal balancing, the yoking, that is the prime identification of a 'ha' 'tha' sun/moon physical asana practice. And so, I spoke about this **all** the time in my classes, always taking my students, and thus *my attention and focus*, to this point. I spoke of the *Ida* and the *Pingala*, the different feminine and masculine energy channels that meet at each of the chakra points running up the *Sushumna* channel of the spine. Of Awakening kundalini energy, allowing us an opportunity to experience a state of consciousness beyond the body and the mind, beyond duality.

In 2017, my dear friend, yogini and stunningly beautiful soul sister, dark curly haired, statuesque former model, Kate, invited me to come to the Eclipse Festival in Oregon, America. I knew nothing about the 'Eclipse' nor the festival, and I hadn't been to America before, but that 'little voice' said to me it was an extraordinary trip to take. Kate and I always had so much fun together. We hadn't known each other in this life for long but were fast and furious friends.

Immediately we 'recognised' one another. We shared the same surname; our fathers shared the same name. I had a blood sister called 'Kate' and we had both journeyed with our mothers to the lifting of the veil because of cancer. Kate was a mystic, and a yoga studio owner, mother of four, fond of flowing feminine 'Rockstar' style clothes worn over cowgirl boots and obligatory yoga pants. We drove each other to hysterics - often. We 'got' one another on all levels. So, I knew the trip would be great anyway, though I wasn't entirely 'convinced' about the festival.

Thus, we took the long haul to America. Did the 'Thelma and Louise' hiring a white Cadillac convertible and drove the majestic drive from San Francisco to Oregon. We went via Mt Shasta in Northern California for a bit of a spiritual sojourn to begin with. Staying in Stewart Mineral Springs, in bear country, bathing in some private crystalline healing mineral baths at the foothills of Parks Creek, Mt Shasta. The energy there was pristine and pure. We felt blessed to spend a few days to recover and replenish from our long trip and were very excited to find a local organic food store. It was such an immensely beautiful place to 'ground' ourselves within a quaint log cabin set amongst massive Californian Red Fir, the continual tinkling of a mystical running stream.

The trip to the Festival was not as smooth and easy for us. We'd paid for early passes so we could enter before the mass crowd. There were about thirty thousand plus expected. We waited in line **all** night in the car on the road with many others. We lined up about five kilometres from the festival, with a local sheriff waking people up every hour or so, to keep the traffic moving if only minutely. The car line was back up all of the way to the local town - creating congestion there. Every hour, upon waking, Kate would start up the car again and we'd move up a couple of spaces in the line, inching closer to the gates of the festival.

It was crazy. We went to the toilet and practiced yoga on the side of the road, pulling our mats out onto the road near the car. Our hire car (we'd swapped to a more sensible four wheel drive) was an overflow of suitcases, escaped clothing and supplies. And we tried to maintain our good humour and excitement.

We finally made it through the gates at about ten o'clock the next morning after being in line and **in the car** for **sixteen hours**. The festival volunteers directed us through a dusty, dirt-infused foetus of a festival to our 'glamping' tents. They'd been advertised as big enough to 'house' two beds, with space to stand in, overlooking the lake, near the showers. Except they weren't. They were in the middle of the dirt, right next to the Portaloos, housing just one double bed, tall enough to stand in if you were a tiny dwarf. And we weren't.

W**e** were unimpressed. The tent had cost Kate almost the price of small island off the Indonesian coast, and this was *definitely not* as advertised. We wandered the festival 'that was a spiritual gathering of all nations', choosing our next move; our eyes inundated with bare breasts and buttocks. These were the garish costumes of young 'festival-goers' in the throes of scoring cocaine, ecstasy, DMT, or marijuana with dust hurtling and screaming its way through into every crease or crevice.

Hmmm. I was definitely wondering what I'd gotten myself into at this point. All seemed absolutely **not** my scene. Well, maybe twenty years ago, but definitely not now. Together Kate and I decided on a course of action to leave and ask the officials for the money back on the not so - 'glamping tent'. Within an hour, we had left the festival in the knowledge of the 'no pass outs allowed, rule' with a half-baked plan of heading back to Mt

Shasta.

We spent a night in the local town, Bend, checking into a cheap franchised hotel. My beautiful friend was distraught. Streams of salty water ran down her face. She'd been looking forward to this for so long. It was her dream. I got in the picture late. The reality wasn't measuring up to her expectations. To exacerbate things, Kate was exhausted after not sleeping at **all** the night before. She'd been the driver. I'd dozed. We ate, and she showered. After showering, she came out.

"I know you will hate me, but how would you feel if we went back tomorrow?" she ventured.

"I won't hate you, Kate. I'm here to support you, but seriously, back to the festival?"

"Yes, well, we can't get back into that nice place in Stewart Springs, and I don't want to go stay in some dodgy place in Weed or Mt Shasta. And I **really** was looking forward to this for ages. Maybe because I was so tired I didn't see things clearly," she explained and partially implored.

I'd had a little more sleep than Kate, and thought I'd seen things pretty clearly, and wasn't too keen to go back. "But where will we sleep? We've said we don't want the glamping tent."

"We can go to Walmart and buy a tent and stuff. It will still be cheaper than what I originally spent," Kate offered.

It was becoming apparent she'd been thinking this angle through with the fresh water cleansing away the dusty remnants of the festival. Meanwhile I'd been hard at googling trying to get us out of there, looking for the best spot to watch the eclipse from.

"Okay, and how will we get back in?" I implored. "They said no pass outs."

"We'll wing it, or talk our way in. It will work. You know we can do this," she reminded me.

Together we were a bit of an unstoppable force.

"Hmmm, okay, **but** only if we don't have to wait in line. I cannot bear to wait in line again. And let's use the mantra, 'I move through life with ease and grace'," I conceded.

After a good night's sleep, we breakfasted on delicious fresh fruit and a smoothie at a healthy local cafe in the small town of Bend. Next came a hilarious time in the local Walmart. We commandeered a shop assistant to assist us in locating a tent, sleeping bags, pillows, and other necessary festival supplies like matching pink and white unicorn onesie's. We repeatedly chanted the mantra of 'We move through life with ease and grace' whenever we found a sticking point. And with 'ease and grace' the sticking point was made moot.

After a hilariously entertaining couple of hours in-store, convincing each other and other customers we had some vestiges of sanity left, we were finally on the drive back into the festival, repetitively chanting our mantra. And we *just drove straight in*. Straight in, no line, no getting stopped despite the 'no pass out rule'. We had a glamping sticker still on the car, and they just waved us directly through, just like we were visiting dignitaries or something.

Once 'in', we drove to look for 'our' camp spot in the direction closest to the VIP section. We were stopped here, our plans a little circumnavigated as we were steered into a family 'camp spot'. Spirit weaved us right under a tree between an Australian family group we'd met on the plane on the way over, and two young and beautiful gay guys from Hawaii. Talk about Blessed. Kate and I were full of so much Gratitude. Then, despite both of us confessing little prowess in tent erection, we managed it, fully complete with a couple of sparkly throws for the 'goddess' flavour within ten minutes. The mantra worked.

We spent the next four days at the festival. The food was excellent and healthy, and there were some fantastic workshops on offer. It wasn't really my vibe, so I spent most of my time photographing people rather than participating. Much loved and revered Australian music duo, Deya Dova, performed one morning, raising the vibration exponentially. This was a zenith moment. Another highlight was to discover the Elders of all Nations, at 1NationEarthcamp holding sessions and space in a sacred camping spot you accessed by 'crossing a literal cultural bridge, above a 52-acre lake.

This was where I found my 'happy spot.' There was no alcohol or other drugs permitted in this area, and respectfully people were asked to be clothed. This formed the literal, spiritual and physical epicentre of the festival. And like the truth of life, you had to make your way through the 'mud' of the festival, to find the 'beauty' and 'Divine.' As the saying goes, 'no mud, no lotus', and this was undoubtedly true. I don't think I ever saw so many penises in my life as I did making my way to the Earth Camp over those four days.

The climax of the festival was the pinnacle moment of the natural phenomenon of the Solar Eclipse. It's what we and so many others had travelled so many miles for. Kate and I formed a procession with the two beautiful gay men we'd camped next to, solemnly and potently playing the drum and flute. We and tens of thousands of others made the long walk to the specially created temple space over the bridge. We passed 1EarthNation Camp on top of the mountain to witness this incredible occurrence in a custom-built area designed for this moment. There were two wooden temples, one honouring the sun, the other the moon.

To begin with, the Original Keepers of the Land, Big Summit Prairie, welcomed us. Then there was a sacred, joyous and solemn ceremony with the Elders of all the nations putting their wishes for humanity into the creative mixing pot. Desires such as All coming together as One, Respecting Pachamumma, living from Love, not Fear. It was so incredibly moving to attest.

Then together with the massive crowd, we all took our gaze trajectory witnessing the sky darkening as the moon covered the sun, with a resplendent 'Om'. We followed this with a reverent silence as together thirty thousand people, viewed through special eclipse glasses, the oscillating wave of the moon dancing with the sun. Through their energetic union, they created an ephemeral undulating movement. We all stood in a unified state of awe, Kate and I moved to tears.

For me, this was witnessing externally on a planetary level what I'd spoken of for years as the ultimate goal of yoga. To bind, to form a union between, the Divine Masculine, the Divine Feminine, the Sun and the

Moon. It was a *pinnacle, life-changing, joyous, monumental* moment of nature to embody. I was overwhelmed, overawed, and full of so much Gratitude for Life itself. *For the Dance of All that Is.*

Then, eight months later, still in awe of what we had witnessed, I was back in Perth practicing and teaching about the Sacred Dance of the Sun and the Moon on the mat. Kate and I offering workshops embodying the essence of what we had been encoded with through the experience, our knowledge had deepened. Spirit then deemed me ready to receive a physical 'bodily' circumstance to experience union between the Feminine and the Masculine. An opportunity to merge with another in a 'creatorship' with a well-loved and respected man from the Perth 'spiritual' scene. After considerable deliberation, I chose to enter the 'dance', and this man and I are both continually expanded through our play. Moral of the story... be careful what you concentrate on, for you are actively bringing it forward to be manifested within this reality.

***

Daily I find, and lose, my Dharana on the mat. Through my asana practice and my meditation practice. My focus wavers between being the observer of my practice and the mind attempting to call me in on some other more 'exciting' endeavour. Reviewing a conversation perhaps, a past happening, or projecting 'me' somewhere in the future. By practicing **only observing** my body, my mind, sometimes even laughing aloud at where it would like me to go, I allow my mind a small sphere with which to work. *Observe the breath, observe the body, observe the mind.* These are the directions and the parameter. This practice helps to evolve my embodiment of pratyahara as does any directive that enables us to focus **entirely** on one thing.

Other examples of where I utilise this skill within my life are when I am professionally capturing moments on my camera or witnessing a majestic tropical sunset. As with all yogic principles, the more we focus on the sadhana on the mat, the more this extends into our lives 'off the mat'. Ultimately, this leads us towards more extended splendiferous moments of **unity** within all things.

Chapter Sixteen
FINDING THAT MASSIVE SPACE WITHIN

Dhyana

Playlist – The Beatles - Across the Universe 1969

In 2010, I attended my first ever yoga festival, the annual 'Bali Spirit', held in Ubud. I was incredibly blessed to go all by myself in my first solitary overseas trip since becoming a parent. My mum and dad took care of my children, and I stayed close to the 'action' in a quaint and inexpensive 'traditional style' Balinese hotel. With plentiful frangipanis and resplendent greenery, my spacious room, overlooking the rice paddies, came with the almost 'arbitrary' tempestuous hot water and leaky toilet. In spite of these Balinese challenges, the hotel allowed me to have ample space to continue my own daily practices.

This was almost eight months into my dedicated practice and 'svadhyaya' of myself, so I was - and still am - finding my way. At the festival, I was a little like a kid in a candy store with a great number of amazing teachers and so many styles of yoga on offer. Over the first couple of days, I practiced five to six, one-hour sessions, with some incredible international teachers, **as well as** doing my hour of asana in the morning and thirty minutes of meditation morning and night. Consequently, by the end of day two, I was exhausted after eight to nine hours of practice; hence, I pulled back a little and offered myself some loving kindness. I recognised the way I was approaching my practice and the Spirit Festival was very yang, lacking ahimsa. I was beating my physical body up, not allowing any room for anything to 'sit' and percolate. I was using my 'single-pointed focus' against myself. The festival goes for a full six days, thankfully with this reflection, I introduced some changes with the way that I experienced things. I backed off a little and met some incredible people, following my intuition, allowing the synchronicity to flow.

One rainy evening after attending three of the assortment of daily sessions on offer with Mark Whitwell, Duncan Wong, and Uma Inder, having cleaned up and done my meditation practice, I ventured back out on a whim for the evening activity's also. Despite my 'all-inclusive ticket' enabling me to attend everything day or night, I'd retired early other nights rather than exploring the evening music or food offerings. In my meditation practice that evening, I had a beautiful, strong, and vivid experience. I connected to the Earthstar, and Soulstar Chakras. These two chakras are thought to exist beyond the familiar seven.

According to the psychiclibrary.com the Earthstar chakra exists below the feet, is usually brown or black in colour. It connects the body to the energies of the Great Mother, and the entire planetary and universal system, holding the key to many past life or karmic connections. The Soulstar chakra is said to be above the crown chakra and instrumental in affecting the balanced feeling of all the other chakras as well as providing clear connection to the higher self. This was to be quite a sentient meditation to experience before making my way through the pouring rain to the eating area at the festival.

***

"Is this seat taken?" a beautiful Eastern lady, standing resplendently in the downpour under her umbrella, asked as she motioned towards the seat next to me. She had the longest blue-black hair I have ever seen.

"No, it isn't. Please sit," I said graciously.

I watched as she gracefully moved her impressively long, ponytail out of the way and sat in the chair, wiping the subtle drops of water from herself. We were sitting in front of a stir-fry stall; they were making the food fresh in front of us. I was still waiting for mine.

"Are you enjoying the festival?" she asked.

"Oh yes, it's amazing," I gushed.

"Are you a yoga teacher?"

I got asked this so many times at the festival it's part of the reason I became one. You only have to hear things so many times to realise that maybe there might be something in it.

"No, I'm actually a videographer," I said.

"Oh, what do you make videos of?" she asked.

"Of people before they die."

"Wow, tell me more."

I explained to her my 'soul work' and we exchanged business cards. Turns out she was a longtime facilitator at Bali Spirit, teaching Quantum Qi Gong[16].

I was astonished, feeling a beautiful rush of 'god-bumps'.

"Earthstar Creations!" I exclaimed incredulously as I read her card. "This is amazing."

I filled her in on the details of my meditation previous to my arrival at the stall.

I was fascinated that I had literally, just an hour prior, been meditating on the 'Earthstar' chakra and here manifested in front of me, so quickly was a physical representation of this very same thing. Important things were underfoot.

"Yes," Ama Lia explained. "The Council of Light instructed me to call my consultancy business that in 1990 as I am to bring in the new

---

16. link to Ama Lia Wai Ching Lee's website www.creative-healing-arts.org www.infintiyquantamqi.com

frequencies."

Ama Lia Wai Ching Lee and I became fast friends after that, both holding the same degree of importance over the magic unfolding of synchronicity. Later that same year, on another trip with my kids, I just happened to be in Bali at precisely the 'right' time to assist her in filming[17] an important event she held in Pura Besakih, the Mother temple of Bali. I was blessed to have Kael and Aala as my assistants. This was their first introduction to the new world that was opening up for me, their initial 'spiritual ceremony' - non religious. Ama Lia's ceremony directly connected with the global work of leading new age interpreter of the Mayan calendar, Carl Johan Calleman. He instigated the creation of a huge planetary 'medicine wheel' through the Conscious Convergence - The Wave of Unity Ceremony movement, calling for satellite ceremonies across the planet. This paves the way forward for the 9th Wave of Human Evolution, thought to come through with the changing of the Mayan Calendar 21st December 2012. It had been foretold that human intention was required to bring this forth into manifestation and this is why it was pertinent to begin to gather groups together in Peace and Unity, prior to. At a stretch, being involved with this highly charged event could be seen to have initially linked me to Joe Collard and the First Nations people here in Western Australia. Remember it co-incidentally began with our first contact on that auspicious date of 21st December 2012. It was certainly interlinked somehow. And I am told by Ama Lia that all forty three of us in attendance at that potent Ceremony, in 2010, received transmissions as she was requested to link us to her work upon the sacred vortices of the planet.

Ama Lia and I will still sometimes catch up when I am over there. Our 'chance' encounter, exemplified in practice for me the power of our dharana - point of focus - and dhyana - meditation, in bringing things forth into physical manifestation. As well as, the magic that is underfoot when you begin activating the feminine brain, the cerebellum, our connection to the cosmic womb, our Awakening Spiritual Heart. Deep

---

17. link to video created for Conscious Convergence https://youtu.be/D0aqcLeJfXI

connection to All that is, thus intuition and our guidance becomes stronger and synchronicity abounds.

Directly after the conclusion of the Bali Spirit Festival, I wisely checked myself into a more upmarket hotel near the ocean in Jimbaran Bay. I had pre-thought to allow myself a couple of days to absorb everything before I went back home to sole-parent my two children, Kael and Aala. I kept to my daily practice of yoga and meditation, and on that very first night I arrived, I had the most incredible session happen. I sat, as usual, spine straight in sukhanasana, easy crossed leg pose, focussed on my breath, and allowed my awareness of my thoughts to dissipate into the void. It was a natural state for me to achieve after having practice so much asana and mediation over the past week. Even with my 'relaxed' state at the festival, I was practicing between five-six hours daily.

***

My consciousness transported me beyond my physical reality, in a place I can only describe as 'up' or 'above' the 'normal' grounded state. Surrounding me was a feeling of incredible infinite field of Divine Love and who I knew to be my Spiritual Guides. I cannot describe them for you as I wasn't aware of seeing them. I was just aware of them being there - a feeling of them. A sense of them if you like. More than one, perhaps four or five. I was having 'flashes' of my experiences thrown into my mind, times when I was behaving senselessly when I was taking so long to learn the lesson. Like my experiences with alcohol, and my guides were laughing, and groaning, saying things like, (which I heard in my head) *"Oh My God and there she goes again. She STILL didn't get it. She goes back in for another round,"* and cracking up laughing. I mean wetting your pants style of laughter. Then I heard them say, *"And look - then we did this - we thought she would get it then BUT NO (more laughter) she still didn't get it."*

I watched each of my lessons as they flashed through, one by one with the speed of light, knowledge dropping in incredibly quickly and I laughed with them. From their perspective, I saw clearly how they'd assisted me and tried to guide me, tirelessly with infinite patience and love. I felt such comradeship with them, such a pure form of Divine love.

They'd been there from the very beginning guiding, or trying to guide my process, whilst allowing me to make my mistakes. Yet they always dropped another bread crumb for me like Little Red Riding hood to pick up in the Forest of Life, showing me and accompanying me along the way. I'd been a little stubborn and a **lot** silly in my learning process. I'd ignored the messages for the most part, and I sat with my guides and laughed and laughed and laughed. We got down to my base message, stripping away all the others, and my most significant lifetime learning of infinite love. That **All** is Love. I remained upbeat and uplifted from this experience for quite some time afterwards, many months. I felt infinitely supported, loved, and forgiven for my 'experiences' up to this point. It provided a strong impetus to continue my movement upwards, wanting to be a better version of me.

I spoke with my mum about this encounter when I got back to Perth, and she found the whole situation very funny. We shared some laughter around some of my lessons, and the whole situation, and it felt like we were moving into a greater space of healing together. We were softening deeper into our relationship together. We agreed this was my biggest lesson all along. That all is love. That we'd come into each other's lives to teach the other about the physical expression of Love, between Mother and Daughter, and the original trinity Father, Mother, and Child. This was so we could understand the ultimate capacity for Infinite love. It was as though the circle magically completed.

* * *

According to Deepak Chopra and David Simon, Dhyana, Patanjali's seventh limb of practice, the limb up from Dhyana, is the pathway to accessing total awareness itself. While frequently referred to as purely mediation, its truth may be as they suggested. The practice of Dhyana is the opportunity to glimpse into the soul, to reach 'Atma darshan' which is entered through the practice of meditation. Such methods of Dharana as Tratarka - candle gazing[18], and Japa mala[19] - chanting with mala beads have assisted me in practicing in this process.

---

18. Link to candle-gazing https://youtu.be/DXxzW4tiMRI
19. Link to japa mala meditation technique https://youtu.be/wGWArKWTnts

When we are practicing Dhyana, it offers us a small glimpse of the whole sea of pure love, Bhakti love, raising, and lifting our vibration. Dhyana allows us the opportunity to be set free, to experience freedom, beyond the body and the machinations of the monkey, often 'child operated' mind, to experience 'moksha.' Freedom. Then we understand we exist beyond the body and the mind, beyond the act of meditating, we become the meditation, as we glimpse a deeper awareness of oneness. Often, the last three limbs, internal in nature, are worked on together, Dharana, Dhyana and Samadhi, in what we term Samyama. The practice of these previous branches, only achievable after following the other five external practices, offers greater insight and is a pathway to higher consciousness. Perhaps this was what I experienced, Samyama, on that beautiful frangipani-filled evening, in the magical and mystical warmth of Bali.

Chapter Seventeen

LIGHTENING THE MIND

Samadhi

Playlist - The Beatles - All You Need is Love 1967

After four years of celibacy, sexual momentum like two trajectories that meet to create velocity came hurling into my life by an enchanting, muscled and mystical, crinkly, zircon-eyed medicine man. He built tipi's, rolled sage, rosemary, eucalyptus, and wormwood smudge sticks, and held full moon drumming sessions. His energy field was like a newborn's. Twice-daily he practiced the ancient Vedic Fire ritual ceremony of Agnihotra[20] at precisely the time of each arc of the sun. It was a dedicated ritual he'd been practicing for twenty-three years, along with a daily yoga 'play'

He was like a 'spiritual cowboy', had used to own and ride horses, playing polo and polocrosse, and lived on a family farm an hour out of Perth. With Pan-essence and Merlin Aspects intermingled with the fine

---

20. link to more information www.agnihotra.org

energetic weave that descendant from the Ascended Masters carries, he held a very high frequency and vibration.

I had known John as a 'brother' and a friend for many years, he is relatively iconic in the Perth Spiritual community.

Until our energetic forces literally collided into each other, I'd always felt for him as a member of my extended 'soul family.' We had worked together from time to time since I moved to Perth. I'd been up to his Traditional Native American Tipi in the hills, made a hoop drum with deerskin, and had also participated in sacred medicine ceremonies with him.

In 2018 though, I recall thinking, 'I'm not sure he sees 'me'.' As the brilliant orange orb dipped beyond the wall of turquoise into the dusky summer sky, as he chanted and beat his drum for one of my yoga sessions, I sent out the precise thought, 'I'm going to lift the veil'. The impact of that directive had resounding implications. The energy electrified, turning into something as fresh as morning dew on jasmine. It was apparent someone had flicked a switch.

Whether co-incidence or not, John began to call me daily. (He will say that he had valid reasons for this. I will say that's debatable). Through our phone contact, I discovered I liked to talk with him. I was enjoying getting to know him better. I wasn't sure why suddenly he was calling me, but I wasn't unhappy that he was. I was secretly delighted. It was exciting, though also creating a bit of inner pandemonium as I began to question my *commitment to* and *reasons for* celibacy.

The timing of this was awkward too. It happened a couple of weeks before impending upcoming international trips in the pipeline for both of us. Him to Damanhur, a spiritual community in Italy, me a yearly re-visit to nourish my soul, in the yoga capital of the world, Rishikesh.

Just days before he was to leave the country, John phoned as I was travelling in my red 'love bug' along a busy double lane road, en route from my hairdresser. I was on my way to teach, and if I didn't fuel up, **right now**, I would probably not make it to the yoga class on time. I'd been on 'Mandi-time' which specifically means I'd already 'borrowed' some time from somewhere.

"Yo, Mandi J."

"John, hey."

"How are you?" we said in unison, then both laughed.

"Yeah, I'm..." We both began and laughed some more.

"You go," he said, still chuckling.

"Okay, well yep, I'm doing okay. Had a pretty relaxing day, been at the beach, just left my hairdresser, on my way to teach yoga. It's a beautiful afternoon, going to be an amazing sunset. What about you?" I responded with a little, nervously excited overflow.

"Yeah, right. You have Julian doing sound tonight, is that right?" he questioned with his drawl.

Julian was a friend and 'brother' to both of us. I'd been working with him for the past five years, or so. He was an incredibly accomplished musician and healer, had spent numerous years with the Aboriginal people, and was a voracious spiritual seeker.

Together we had birthed wildly popular 'Tribal yoga' - a yoga asana-dance fusion embracing sacred ceremony. The underlying principle was to help cultivate respect and honour to the indigenous cultures of the world, in particular, the Australian Aboriginals. Our co-creations together were always well received, and we did many sound and yoga healing experiences together, positively impacting many people.

"Yeah, I'm looking forward to it. It will be good. Julian is great to work with. What about you?"

"Yeah, well, umm... I'm not really sure how to say this... I mean, I don't really know anything about you."

"What are you talking about?" I said, glancing at the time the dash of my VW and recognising I was definitely running short of it, as well as petrol. The understanding 'dropping in' that I couldn't talk on my phone and fuel up at the same time hit me. I was in a conundrum. My interest in this conversation *was* ignited, *though* if I didn't keep moving, then I would miss my class.

"Well, you see this thing happened today, this morning."

I could sense John was finding it difficult to get his words out, which was a little unusual as his flow was akin to a shower with the tap set to on. Good to go. Feels delicious, though sometimes it can get stuck and is difficult to turn off.

"I don't even know where to start, really, and I know nothing about you. I've been having it go around in my head all day, and I think I should tell you, then I think I shouldn't."

"I think you should," I said apprehensively, yet encouragingly. Time was not on our side, and I was almost at the closest service station, without the option to skip it for the next one. I was almost completely out of fuel by now.

"Well, the thing is, like I don't even know what your status is, like if you are in a relationship if you are into men or women or what?"

"Mm, well I'm not in a relationship," I responded with a tingled gulp. I feel for a moment time seemed to stop as we began to head into one of those weird space and time stretch moments. "And I'm into men, but you need to know I'm celibate and have been so for the past four years."

"You're celibate? Wow... what? Okay, so is that one of those experiment things you are doing - taking a vow for ten years like you did with alcohol?" John's voice raises a little.

"No, I haven't placed a time limit on it, it's part of my spiritual practice. I hadn't considered how long I was committing for because there hasn't really been anyone I seriously contemplated what it might mean to me to let go of." I responded from my heart. I'd spent so long on cleansing and purifying my system, my body, my mind, making amends, I wasn't interested in getting involved with '**anyone**'. I couldn't go back through the messiness of drugs or alcohol via a partner, didn't want to have to 'teach' someone the 'ropes' concerning the spiritual work I'd been doing.

I'd only ever contemplated an end to celibacy *might be a consideration*, if I met a person who was at least at the level, if not beyond me spiritually, so maybe I could learn from them. It would have to be a conscious relationship, with sacred lovemaking, and benefit both people as a place from which to grow. Someone out of the 'matrix,' interested in yoga or daily 'watering of their temple', spiritual growth and walking that path together. Someone clean on every level. I'd spent so long on my path to purification, eight and a half years to be precise, the last thing I wanted to be doing was travelling that same path with a partner. Or 'cleaning' them in bed overnight as my human system, as a 'projector' was designed to do.

To be honest, I had thought I'd find 'it'- as in a possible partner, on an overseas trip - if one was ever going to arise. I didn't think I would find 'it' in Perth. John had been in a long-term relationship that had ceremonially concluded just over four months previously.

And I just pulled into a service station, though it felt we were in a 'warp'. I was running out of time to have this conversation or petrol.

"Well, I'm still not sure that I should tell you, part of me thinks it should the other part thinks not…" He continued to deliberate.

Hurry up, Johnny, I'm thinking. I'm parked at a petrol station stationary, waiting to hear what feels like some very vital, life-altering information. I feel I can't hang up because I can't handle the suspense. I can't get out of the car because I'll ignite the whole fuel station. Immobilised, I can't drive any further because my vehicle just won't drive any further without me feeding it some more fuel. And to top it off, I can't sit here any longer because every precious moment counts, **and** I need to get to my yoga session to meet Julian and my students.

"Anyway, then after lunch, I went for a swim in the dam, and as I was walking up to the house it just dropped in. I should just ring Mandi J and tell her, and I still don't…"

"John, I'm sorry I've interrupted you. I think you **do** need to tell me whatever it is you are wondering about telling me- **but** - the thing is I have to cut this conversation short."

"Oh, that's okay. It probably wasn't a good idea to share it with you anyway."

Oh My God, I thought, NOOOOOO!

"No, I **want** to hear what you are about to say. I'm incredibly torn. I've been sitting here at the petrol station a couple of minutes anyway, **but I have** to get petrol right away, because if I don't, I won't make it to yoga on time. So, let me get petrol then I will call you back, **straight** away and you can tell me, okay?"

John was notoriously tricky to get hold of via telephone. Actually tricky to get hold of 'any' way except in the person. He'd only recently transitioned to a mobile phone from the landline. He lived on a five hundred and fifty-acre family property in the hills, an hour out of the metropolis. Being 'engaged' to media and communications wasn't part of his world as it was mine. And thus, you just couldn't be sure when you would be next guaranteed to get hold of him. It was almost like waiting for all the planets to form a particular alignment.

"Yeah, okay."

"Great, I'll call you back in five minutes or so."

I filled the car up with a quick twenty dollars, and literally ran in and paid the cashier, full of nervous anticipation, sensing he was about to tell me something **Big**. I couldn't even imagine what he would say. We had been communicating daily, sure. My girlfriends, my sisters, *my Dad* also, and I'd been behaving a little like I was a teenager again, analysing **the** conversations with me.

'Is he interested or not?' 'Is he calling me as a 'brother' daily?' 'Do I even want to break my celibacy?' 'If I'm to break my celibacy, is it with him?' 'Does he fit the criteria?' 'Am I ready for this?' 'He is very sexy.' 'He definitely has a thing.'

He had **definitely** been the topic of more than **one** conversation. Suddenly I was spending a lot of my time on the phone.

I took a deep breath, plugged my earphones in my ears, put my car into drive, foot almost slipping off the accelerator, and phoned him back in four minutes and forty-five seconds flat. I wouldn't allow him to get called away from the phone out onto the property doing whatever job he was working on somewhere on the land. Mobile range was not reliable on the property, and to keep him in one spot inside the house so that he could answer the landline took quite an effort.

A little nervously, I heard the phone dialling once, twice, then…

"Mandi J."

"John."

"I still don't know if this is a good idea, though I'll tell you what happened," he said quickly.

"Okay," I said apprehensively. "Go ahead." I now had fifteen minutes' drive up my sleeve.

"Well, you know how I do Agni-hotra fire ceremony every morning at sunrise and every evening at sunset," he began.

"Yes." (Well, kind of.)

"So, this morning I did a beautiful fire, got right on time, and had the red tail and the whitetail cockatoos fly over as I was playing the flute."

"Oh wow, sounds so beautiful."

"It was really special and really magical. And then, as I lay down on my back as I do straight after Agni and I do a bit of a stretch from side to side, a vision of you dropped in."

I felt the wings of a delicate baby bird in my heart begin to unravel.

"And it was literally like you were there. Like I wasn't just imagining you or anything. I didn't think of you, and then you came in… You were this apparition… a vision… Like you teleported or something, and you were nude, straddling me, and moving sensually, in a tantric way, and then there were dragons."

"There were dragons," I managed. Let alone the rest of it that I was attempting to digest. Those wings in my heart now vibrated a little.

"Yeah, well, you know about my whole story with Dragons, don't you?" he continued. "You know how my email is dragon based, and I had this whole journey with dragons showing up everywhere about ten years ago. And then what happened this morning, we turned into a green dragon and a gold dragon intertwining and spiralling up and out of the top of the tipi together in a flame of love."

"Right okay."

I was trying to get my head around all of it. It was a lot to ingest. I wasn't sure what it all meant, what he was trying to tell me by sharing this vision he'd had. And he was talking to a celibate woman. I hadn't had intimate conversations with men for a while. And could honestly say never any that involved entwining dragons. Or manifestations. Or me teleporting.

And then there was the fact I'd woken up feeling sensual, almost as if I'd engaged in some kind of lovemaking. I'd thought I'd dreamed. These were not usual feelings for me to regularly have in my period of celibacy. It had probably occurred on a handful of occasions over the timespan.

"Well," I said, "it gets more interesting because a couple of weeks ago when I was with Aboriginal Elder, Nanna Violet and her consociate, Michael. They bought through my green dragon and in this visualisation, the green dragon meets a gold dragon… and they kind of meld into a union."

"I'm the gold dragon," he said.

"Oh wow. This is amazing, John. I don't know what to say."

I was dumbstruck. This was all getting very weird, and 'out there', very quickly. And I know weird I've been it most of my life.

"Mandi J, this is a-m-a-zing," he said.

"It truly is. I have some more to share with you on this, but I've arrived at my class. Can we talk later?"

"Sure thing, call me later."

"Okay. Wow! Okay… and thank you, John, for sharing this with me. I know it would have taken some courage."

"Thank you, Mandi J, for hearing me."

I'd like you to take your mind to a place where you see a bomb going off inside an unknown car. And it seems it just happened that you were standing in close enough distance to be swept up in the fracas. Shuttled through the air, the lightening-white light blinds you as it penetrates and infiltrates every cell, molecule and atom of your body. Time and space seem to disappear within your trajectory. You are weightless until you land cushioned in a luscious Istanbul velvet daybed set in a Californian bloom of springtime, your senses all heightened and **awake**…

Got that? Okay, so that's kind of where I was at as I walked into meet Julian and teach that class.

With those wings quivering noticeably.

***

John and I ended up speaking later, and I bravely shared with him the part about how I had awoken that morning. We were both reasonably thunderstruck by the unfolding of the events. And also, we both were individuals guided by synchronicity and Spirit's hand. So, it seemed there was a 'thing' there. I began to feel urges I'd denied for a long time. We communicated by phone a couple of times a day before we each left the country for the best part of the next month.

I would have loved to have seen him before he left, but he was just unable to squeeze it into his schedule. The two-hour distance travel time had to be factored in and this just didn't allow for a face to face catch up prior to our departures. And he hadn't been away for twenty years or so, so getting him off his land was taking a bit. Let's tell it like it was, **a lot**.

While away, daily, we emailed beautiful long narrations of how our days had flowed and how the 'other' was prevalent in our lives. These were delicious morsels of art, masterfully crafted and cared for, expressions of an exquisite budding flower of love. Those wings in my heart began to open and expand. There were so many magical, synchronistic moments where I would experience what he was experiencing by merely closing my eyes and 'connecting in' - focussed thinking of him.

One time, I found I had a particular mantra chant running through my head. As I walked the vibrant sensory streets of Rishikesh, smells of sweet incense interspersed with fresh cow dung, and rich aromatic spices, with the big question of Love within my heart, I heard it. Which isn't a weird thing in Rishikesh because the streets are almost littered with them.

"Jay Shiva Shankara Bom Bom Hare Hare, Jay Shiva Shankara Bom Bom Hare Hare, Hare Hare Bom Bom Hare Hare, Hare Hare Bom Bom Hare Hare."

When I was reading John's latest email, it turns out he, six hours' time difference away in the foothills of the Alps in the Chiusella Valley in Italy, had been chanting this at the same time. That was the synchronicity.

Another time, while dear friend, Dawn, and I were flying over to Rishikesh together. It was getting close to the exact equinox time as we were almost twelve hours into our twelve and a half hour flight. I told her I would close my eyes and meditate to 'connect' in with the energy of the equinox and the sacred ceremony being held in Damanhur. She said she would do the same, so we closed our eyes and meditated for about fifteen minutes or so, throughout the exact equinox timing.

Suddenly, I had a vision of lightning hitting a tree, and both I and Dawn, *who had no knowledge of my vision*, were both simultaneously thrown forcibly into the backs of our seats. When I recounted that via email to John, he told me the focus for their ceremony had been around the Mother tree. Perhaps the focussed energy was surrounding the Mother tree right at this time. Maybe this was the energy that we connected in with and felt as we travelled through the skies.

Despite **all** the infinite magic unfolding between us, I was still asking the universe for signs and messages as to what decision was best for me, and for the Highest Greater Good, regarding John. I communicated about it regularly with Dawn with whom I was sharing a room. She was privy to some of our emails, swooning in all the 'right' spots, trying to assist me in coming to some decision. It was a massive deal for me to give up my celibacy. It was a sadhana and a very substantial gift to the person I offered that too. I asked the Goddess Ganga (Ganges) as I bathed in her icy cold, translucent aquamarine waters. I asked the brown, wizen-faced orange-robed sadhus I bought chai for from the haphazard local well-worn cart stand. My heart called out to the majesty and vastness of Kunjapuri Temple in the Himalayas in the crystallised golden morning light.

Unknown to me, Shiva had left a piece of Sita's body there after she died at the feet of her father, the extension of the story of the namesake of my favourite pose - Virabradhasana - Warrior 2.

The pose in my sadhana I'd always found my questions, my answers and the essential sense of the truth of myself. I asked with my prayers and my mantra, in my chanting with the Hare Krishnas who I spent much time within Perth, offering Seva (service) through media work. And I quested through my sadhana on the mat. I *tuned* into my beautiful, vulnerable, incredibly fragile, right at the point of blooming unfurling, undulating, unfolding, awakening, expansive Heart. To those wings that wanted to fly.

Are you ready for this? resounded repetitively through the echoing chambers of my temple.

Eventually, India assisted me in finding the clarity of my understanding. I'd committed to celibacy because I thought it could offer me the path for *most significant spiritual growth at that point in time*. It was part of my path of purification. Now I was at a fork in the road. And it was clear that a new path was being forged for me. And it seemed Spirit played a hand in this. The Signs were all there. I decided if I didn't follow this exploration of our connection through with John, it might be one of those things I regretted on my Graduation from Life. And I'm not one to leave regrets.

***

It was a whirlwind upon both of us arriving home. There was some clearing to be done, and together, John and I embarked upon a journey in what esteemed international channeller, Rebecca Dawson, said was a meeting of the Earth and the Sky. Our 'immediate' union ruffled some feathers in the community, though it was widely celebrated, took some adjusting to for many including us. We were both going through so many processes integrating our individual spiritual initiations from our trips, and the combination of our energies. It was an intense time of dissolving of the old. One day as we were driving together in the car, John tells me he had a 'moment' as he glanced across at me.

He thought, 'Who am I?' Then, 'Who are you?'

This type of thing was prevalent throughout our 'creator-ship,' an intense period of *dissolution of self*. And there were many times initially and sometimes still, when driving out of his long driveway, I didn't think I dared to go back. Understanding my fear, and that Love can heal all, I moved into his place within a couple of months, moving out on my two children, then twenty-one and seventeen. They remained living with Conor, my former partner from whom I'd been renting the upstairs apartment.

It was a quick, sudden, massive change, formula race style, and there is so much to write about this time and moving forward it could be the subject of my next book. We were Gifted the most magical of experiences through our lovemaking - shapeshifting - changes of perceptions - changes of ages - kundalini awakenings - it had all the glitter and sparkle of the Stars. It was the dance of Shakti with Shiva, Divine Union, tantric in nature, without aspiration to be. The deep exploration into the Divine Feminine and Divine Masculine for both of us. And any of these experiences I could question as '*Samadhi*', though probably understand them more to be that of '*Ananda*' - Deep Bliss.

We went to a tiny romantic island off Bali for a seven-day break, four months into our union to find some space, to honour one another, and ourselves. We spent long and languorous days, lizards in the sun, making love, feasting upon ripe, rich and juicy tropical fruits, and eating organic foods. We performed sacred fire rituals on the beach at sunset, where John played the Native American Flute. It mesmerised me. His music spoke to the yearnings of my heart that had not yet been articulated. I was a cup overflowing Santosha.

One particular day, we'd been making love in our private pool in the villa we were staying in, with no intention, or finish line in mind. We were just being conscious and focused in our every movement. We stopped and moved out of the pool to sit cross-legged facing one another, eye-gazing, meditatively, without physically touching.

In the space between us, a light show magically transpired, hundreds and thousands of golden light molecules glittering and dancing between us. Time stood still and warped. There was only Love. Everything was Love. We were All Love. There was no separation between us because there was no separation that existed in this Consciousness. This was the Unified Conscious field, and we were **all** one within it. Within this Unified Conscious field, there was only pure Divine Love. The Collective Consciousness. This felt like infinite creation. The word that came to mind was Samadhi.

The Eighth Limb of Patanjalis sutras.

According to Swami Veda, in its purest form Samadhi is a Sanskrit word made up of three parts. 'Sam' 'a' and 'dhi' formed from the root 'dha.' 'Sam' means altogether, 'a' meaning from all sides, 'dha' which means to place or possessing. So, putting all of those magical Sanskrit words in a collaboration means 'everything from all sides, placed together in one moment of consciousness, with no more differentiation left.' I am also aware it means Supreme Bliss, Ultimate Bliss, Super Consciousness. Many years ago, when I first considered the meaning of the word, the English equivalent bandied around was 'Enlightenment'. I got the impression it didn't happen to everyone, only to sages and the like, not something really to aspire to within this lifetime.

Then as my sadhana deepened over the years along with my understanding of yoga, with still so far to go, I came across a belief I really resonated with. If the English interpretation of the word 'enlightened' is studied, via Latin derivative, it means 'into light.' If 'ment' is broken down, we find the definition is the mind. Therefore, another more 'user-friendly' way to hold this word to our Awakening Spiritual Hearts is to think of it as a 'Lighting of the Mind.' Bringing more light to the mind. A path I'd been *dedicatedly* walking for almost the best part of a decade.

That sublime omnipresent experience involved a partner, to alight the flame of the feminine, Shakti, back within me, to coax it back to its strong fiery resonance until its dance matched that of his own. Through the undulation of the Universal poles of Separation we found the ultimate union for life itself within this expression. And yoga means 'to yoke' or 'union.' It's probably fair to divulge that this was not any partner for me, though one that has been coined as a 'Twin Soul.' This is not a state I'd previously experienced, and I am unsure if the learning could have taken place without John playing his part. By myself, it may have been a little like 'rubbing myself at the hipbone and wondering why I was never coming to orgasm.' Would have been a very long journey.

***

We both drew much from that experience. We felt Magnificently Blessed with another Stunning Sacred, Seraphic experience that our togetherness of this 'creator-ship' had bought forth into manifestation. Another incredible Gifting was a mudra, used to 'clear' the body with Dragon's Breath.

I want to emphasise it's not my intent to 'display' this as an 'exclusive' way to achieve Samadhi if that is in fact what John and I shared together. I have read there are **many** unique experiences of Samadhi, and it concerns me that people might feel you need a partner to access this. It seems at that point it was what I required. Though I feel it necessary to mention I did also experience a similar 'Ananda' or 'Samadhi' type of experience a couple of months later.

It happened while involved in a mantra chanting course led by International Mantra teacher, Anandra George, at The Sound Temple up in the Perth hills. We had been chanting "Om Namah Shivaya" for almost an hour, and she encouraged us to 'let go,' and I did. Again, an almost indescribable beyond the mind, beyond the body, extraordinary experience of my heart being the expression and at One with the whole universe and there was no Separation. I floated in Blissful awareness, a spiralling piece of starlight in the Divine Collective Consciousness.

Both were 'peak' *beyond feeling* human experiences. Just as that meditation was I shared in the last chapter in Bali. All three contain the elements of Samyama - the concentration, the meditation, and bringing it all together back to where we originally began. The critical thing to note was *I never set out with the goal in mind to reach Samadhi.* John and I are 'open' to the exploration with no purpose or destination in sight. A little like making love without chasing the orgasm. You just explore for the sake of experimentation, to express and Be love. To connect. When I gaze back over my lifetime, I recognise I am very fortunate to have had many weird and wonderful 'events' that have shown up on my timeline. I am pleased to say I have witnessed that they definitely **are** of a **much** more refined nature since I began refining myself. These are the realms and fields I have explored and play in to discover new things about my 'Self', my external world, and the planetary world. What *incredibly exciting and challenging work t*o be engaged in. The path of 'Questing and Exploring, Uncovering and Unravelling, getting to Play at being all of those fantastic 'superheroes', those incredibly enticing mystical creatures we knew existed even after we closed the book and our eyes as a kid. This is only the very basics of what we can explore upon this planet.

* * *

In the very second line of the one hundred and ninety-six of Patanjali's sutras is quite a famous, well-utilised line by many Western yoga teachers.

"Yogas citta vritti nirodhah."

While there are many translations or interpretations of the text, referring to moving the fluctuations of the mind, there is one relevant to what we have been unravelling. 'Yoga is the process of ending the definitions of the field of consciousness.'

Flipped into Present Consciousness-

Your

Own

God

Awareness

is the process of Beginning to Explore **Beyond** the definitions of the field of Consciousness.

May You journey well, Beautiful Shiny One.
You are Ready.

AFTERWORD

Writing this book has been quite the process. You could say it's been in the birthing canal from the moment I emerged between my mother's legs. Stretching and as stiff as a board having been cramped in her tiny belly for almost nine months. I've been compiling stories and experimenting for that long. I was given a Directive from 'Source' around the age of twenty-two that I knew at some point I would write a book. I also knew it had to be completed by the time of fifty revolutions around the sun. So I left it right up until I was forty-nine to begin to write it…

My beautiful mirror and partner, John, and I both started writing our books in the most idyllic spot ever in Koh Phangnan, in September 2018. We were there for three and a half weeks, and out of nineteen writing days, I purged forty thousand words from my heart to this format. We were so blessed to stay in Swami Pujan and Betty's place, a couple I'd met on training at Byron Yoga Centre many years before in Byron Bay. The very first morning we awoke here I realised; it was just as I'd visualised through a session with a therapist in drug rehab back in the day. Right down to being able to see the ocean upon awakening from the four-poster bed, and the man laying next to me. In my vision, I did my yoga sadhana and then wrote as I overlook the lapis lazuli waters of the infinite ocean for four to five hours a day. And so it was.

Those initial forty thousand came hurling out, fast and furious. It was so beneficial to head straight into the water, just twenty metres away, on our private beach, to cleanse in the saltwater straight away. John reckons he could see the visible change upon my pallor and expression when it had been a particularly 'tough' session to go through. And it felt really safe to have his masculine strength with me as he sat writing at his own space a floor below me, to allow my vulnerability to seep through these downloads. He enabled me to have the courage to re-walk many of these paths I'd left way behind.

As Above, So below. I know at times I have been challenging to hold. I salute you for your Infinite patience, my Love. You are the Shiva to my Shakti, the yang to my yin, the Sun to my Moon. Together we are Cosmos in Union - the Earth Meeting the Sky. Thank you for your hot lemon drinks, overflowing smoothies, your spontaneous gifts of Nature upon the pillow or in my car, for always getting me out of the door, and started each morning.

There was no space in my busy little life to write any further over the next six months. I taught at many festivals, held lots of public yoga, meditation and healing events, and picked up lots of photography work over the sunny season. Then we took a group of twelve to my soul-space, Rishikesh, in India for a nine day retreat. That required a little recovery from.

The next part of the book was written between May and June intermittently between other commitments and responsibilities. Chasing the warmth of the sun around the back lawn at 'our' peaceful and sacred, high energy place in Gidgegannup, at a top-secret hideaway destination gifted for me to use at Dunsborough. (You know who you are - from the depths of my heart I thank you - for everything - always.) Here I was again treated to the most beautiful view of our turquoise blue Indian Ocean as I 'downloaded' and waded my way through the muddy terrains of my life. Then I wrote the last little bits at Conor's place.

My dogs and my kids, my stepchildren and some or all of their friends, my former partner, and John all naturally rolling in and out as the waves do with the shore.

It was interesting to visit my chiropractor, Sonia, as I'd been working on the chapters of gang rape and drug detox. She'd asked me if I was okay and suggested perhaps I was carrying some trauma from my clients. When I questioned why, she informed me my pelvis was out as if from violent sex and my kidneys and liver were going through detox! Ah, what an amazing, intelligent design this human body is! So of course, there was more clearing to be done.

Emotionally, spiritually, physically the re-telling of some of these stories has been incredibly challenging. I've had to 'go back there' to write authentically, and many of these tales are from 'evolutions' of Mandi ago. I've been through so much personal growth through this. I've had white fire coursing through my veins for days, fevers, realisation after realisation, much of it quite awkward and embarrassing to have to 'fess up to myself about.

I have Infinite Gratitude for my Sensational Seven, the beautiful Earth Angels who are always there for me as Guiding Lights showing me the way back home. On the end of the phone, or face to face, Wonder-woman, Kate Nelson - sister of my soul, I can hear your cheers from here and we live literally an hour and a quarter away from one another on our closest days! Christine Morrison - for her sisterly mothering, her caring and Deliciousness with Sound. The individualised specific music she did for me, to help me complete this book and the healings she gifted me, her continual encouragement of my wounded heart, to grow, to be courageous, and to continue and finish.

To my unpaid 'Life coach' Sydney Sarah Berenice, for your words of infinite wisdom, thank you for 'hearing me' and 'seeing me' so clearly, for beckoning me forth with this project.

To Dawn Steele, to think that trip to India would be so monumental - huh? Thank you Beautiful one for all of your support, always!

I love you my beautiful sis-stars.

To my Brother Julian, similarly a voice on the other end of the phone, who must have thought I'd lost the plot a couple of times with the randomness of my behaviour or conversation. I felt your Light. Thank you, my Brother. And I feel so blessed to have worked together for so many years - you are a sound alchemist!

And last but no means the least the two who continually encourage me to grow and evolve spiritually, daily, my Beloved Nanna Violet, and Michael.

I bow at your feet in Love, Grace, Honour, and Respect. Infinite Gratitude.

There are many other 'angels' that have encouraged my evolution and exploration of Self, that either regularly support my work and growth, or have done in the past. Helen Duke right at the very beginning of my #10yearexpereiment, back in Margaret River, Jo Harvey and Robbie Hamilton from Yoga tree Perth where I teach regularly, and I did most of the filming - thank you for allowance and celebration of me. Heartfelt Gratitude to Rebecca Schelfhout from Mums On A Mission, Alison Jarrad, Kali Ma Shub, the late Shane Moody, Sandi Hancock, Stuart Watkins, Rebecca Dawson, the late Neills Scott and my mum's yoga teacher, Margaret Willcocks. With Love and Gratitude to Ana Forrest and Jose Calarco, two inspirational humans whom have become friends. I just love your work - and feel so blessed for your support of me!

To all of my beautiful kids, Kael, Aala, Clare and Freya… what can I say? I'm one of 'those' mums. Thank you for choosing me. I so enjoy observing each of your Earth walks. And you all inspire me to be more. I am so very proud of each of you.

To Conor, we shared the most incredible story over the past fifteen years. I have so much respect for you and all that you give and have given. I'm proud of us. We've come such a long way.

And Infinite gratitude for my Dad, Rob Nelson for the numerous car conversations of support, and for originally leading the way forward for me. For your lessons of 'consequences' that fell across deaf ears, and for encouraging us to think beyond 'the sheep' mentality. Lastly, for urging me continually just to experiment to see what life might be like without alcohol. You were right. I love you.

And to my sister Melanie, who led me to the Light when I was right in the pit of my cave, many years ago followed me around in clubs in the city, keeping me decent, pulling my skirt down, so I wasn't showing my knickers. Thank you for being my co-pilot in the early formative years as we explored these terrains together. Still saving you that spot - right next to me, for when you are ready.

Mum, I love you. I felt you too. You were there with me as you are now and always. You are within me, and I am an expression of you. Infinite

Gratitude for all you Gifted me with this lifetime. I'm so glad we chose each other. We taught each other so well.

Acknowledging my brother Garth, you ratbag! I'm sorry my direction was the wrong way to begin with, so pleased we are on the right path, in varying degrees of alignment these days! And Kate, you have taught me so much, I thank you. Love you both.

To Aunty Sue. Thank you. Always a Shining light upon my path, supporting, holding and nourishing my spiritual development. Abundant Love.

To Garry & Di, Bec & Rach, thank you for providing my 'second home' for a number of years through adolescence & assisting in healing my heart intermittently throughout my life. Love our interweave through one another's lives, always showing up in pivotal moments. Thank you for your 'forever' support.

With infinite gratitude to the synchronicity that led to the meeting and subsequent incredibly meaningful relationship that developed between Joe Collard and I. Joe, I thank you for your acceptance, forgiveness and for having the courage to entrust me. The healing we have generated from our connection resonates infinitely across all of the universe. With all of my heart I thank you my friend.

Just before the commencement of writing this book, I had a forty-ninth ceremony. We held it at our place in the hills, in John's Tipi, and I invited 'special' people to me in my life to attend. I was Blessed to have Alison Jarrad hold space. We had a candle for each of the seven by seven revolutions, an opportunity for me to speak about what I had to let go from that time and what I had harvested. Then everyone in the circle got to say some words about me. It was such an honouring, humbling experience that provided the initial boost for me to see this Directive through.

Also, there are so many other beauty-filled people within my life who I would like to thank, but too many to name. To all of those who have offered me words of gentle encouragement along the way. To those that have contributed to my spiritual growth, however small or large. They've enquired after the book's whereabouts, provided a touch, a smile, a connection with me of some sort, infinite love and gratitude. I include every one of my students, for having the discipline to show up to yourself each day and each week. For your commitment and dedication. For going along with my weird and wacky ideas and experiments, for co-creating, the events that Spirit 'drops' in and I, with a bit of help from my friends, and studio owners bring forth into manifestation. Without you, I am not a teacher.

Big Love and Gratitude to my main man on the Ground, Craig Whalley. You are a legend. You appeared out of nowhere and just started helping, studying, learning, and growing. I see and recognise your Seva, my dear friend, and I thank you with all of my heart - you make the way for me so much clearer.

Acknowledgement to Kez Wickham St George - the first reader of the full manuscript, for her feedback and encouragement! To then, the journey that unfolded through Joanne Felder and Natasha Gilmour, both of who rallied my efforts and directed me through to the ultimate fit, Making Magic Happen, Karen McDermott. A magic circle unfolded even in that process. Thank you Karen. Immediately you were 'on board' and have supported my many requests with infinite love, in amongst your six kids and dental surgery with my omnipresent demanding timeline! We connected straight away. I felt safe with you. And much appreciation for enlisting Dannielle Line, the beautiful editor I'm yet to meet face to face. Our souls have entwined though, and I am so grateful for your work in helping me to refine my work and my voice.

Last but not least to you the Reader. Thank You for sharing your Time and Energy with me, in this Space. You made it. Take a deep breath. Then do it. Go Create the Life you were born to Live.

In Lakesh

EPILOGUE

There is one last tale I would like to share with you before this transmission ends. It refers to 'stories' and possibly, it provides a culmination to some of the stories I have shared with you from my life, to exemplify the Eight limbs of yoga. The 'stories' that we all have to a greater or lesser degree impacting our lives and how we 'operate' within the world. Each time we open our mouth a 'story' comes out, and the way we choose to tell these depends upon our particular perspective at that time. And on who is 'operating' the machinery - our child, or our adult.

John and I were at home at opposite ends of the bath, a couple of months into our creator-ship. A friend of his had visited before I returned from my couple of days absence teaching down in the city. We were catching each other up on our days, gently stroking one another as the heat of the water massaged our tired and aching bodies.

John yawned. "Yeah, so then Corey dropped in, and we had a bit of chat, and then I started to get dinner ready."

But that isn't what I heard, and I was instantly triggered. I'd heard, "Yeah, so then Corey dropped in, and we had a drink, and then I started to get dinner ready."

Initially, living with a partner who on a rare occasion would have a drink of alcohol was an issue for me. It came down to all of my stuff around purification, walking the same path, and fear of entity attachment. We had a loose agreement of staying on the same wavelength if I was going to be around, and John had known I was coming home tonight after a couple of nights away. For those of you who know anything about gene keys, I'm a 'forty-nine' which basically means one of my shadow behaviours is "reaction," and this is what I struggled with. I was 'trigger-happy."

I felt the emotion rise through my body from my solar plexus to my head, blood coursing with ferocity to my brain, my fiery mouth about to explode with flames I couldn't bring back.

Slowly I said, "What did you just say then?"

John repeated, "Oh look, love, I don't know. Didn't I just tell you Corey dropped in, and we had a bit of chat, and then I started to get dinner ready?"

"So you said nothing about having a drink?"

"No," John said and looked a little bewildered. "What are you talking about? Why would I have a drink when I knew you were coming home, my love and I haven't seen you for so long?"

I let out the biggest exhalation of my life.

"Oh MY GOD, Goddess and All that is."

The profoundness of the situation hit me. I was being thrown off, catapulting down a really large skyscraper. And with my descent, all the 'stories' of my life, all the times my mind found 'fact' to support the emotional trigger of rejection and fear, my whole life, swirled around me in a whirling motion. One after another, story after story, chapter after chapter, page after page, sentence after sentence, word after word, they swirled around me until I felt horribly nauseous.

My whole perspective on my reality experienced a tilt.

My 'truth' had been knocked upon its own head. Consequently, I was no longer sure of the Truth. About anything.

I had been Gifted a new perspective of Reality. I couldn't help wondering how many times in the past, my Perspective had been disparate to reality.

And then I let that go, practicing Aparigrapha and surrendered, practicing Ishvara Pranidhana. Connected back in with my breath.

It was all just an Experience anyhow.

THE END

DISCOVERY LIST

- Brian Swimme 'Journey of the Universe'
- Ana Forrest www.forrestyoga.com
- Richard Rudd GeneKeys - www.genekeys.com
- Patanjalis Yogs Sutra's
- "The Heart of Yoga" TVK Deskichar
- Sri Swami Sivananda in the 'Practice of Bramacharya' (1934)
- 'Light on Yoga' BKS Iyengar
- 'Light on Pranyama' BKS Iyengar
- 'Tibetan Book of the Dead' Bardo Thodol
- 'Autobiography of a Yogi' Paramhansa Yogananda
- 'Bring Yoga to Life' Donna Farhi
- 'Zen and the Art of Motorcycle Maintenance' Robert M Persig
- Bhagavad Gita - so many translations
- Julian Silburn - www.soundalchemy.com.au
- Kate Nelson - www.fremantleyoga.com
- Rebecca Dawson - www.rebeccadawson.net
- Anandra George - www.truefreedomcoaching.com
- Christine Morrison - www.christinemorrison.com
- http://yogachicago.com/2014/03/swami-veda-on-samadhi-the-mind-and-world-peace/
- Monier-Williams Sanskrit-English Dictionary
- The Sound Temple - www.thesoundtemple.com.au
- Deya Dova - www.deyadova.com
- Kali Ma Shub - www.kaliearthma.com
- Sandi Hancock - Yoga Moon Margaret River
- The Margaret River Yoga School

- Kim Echammaal www.kimechammaal.com
- 'Womb Awakening: Initiatory Wisdom from the Creatrix of All Life' Azra & Seren Bertand 2017
- 'Yoga of Heart' Mark Whitwell
- 'The Promise of Love, Sex and Intimacy' Mark Whitwell
- Byron Yoga Centre www.byronyogacentre.com
- Tiara Kumara www.Iamavatar.com
- Joe Collard www.birrdiya.com
- Alison & Graeme Jarred www.consciousunity.info

ABOUT THE AUTHOR

A decade ago, Mandi J Nelson dusted herself off, deciding to become the 'Best Version of herself,' embarking upon an initial ten-year experiment. In earnest, she began a 'path of purification,' actively choosing growth at every juncture. A Golden Key Honour recipient, she is a teacher, photographer, healer, funeral celebrant, spiritual mentor and writer. Her 'soul work' is to film the terminally ill before they die. Mandi J is passionate about the Sun and Moon, Ceremony, Original People, and Cacao in the Tipi. She commutes between the city and the country, her children, students, Beloved, soul family, and her dogs. Following the sun across the globe, she holds pilgrimages to spiritually charged destinations, lovingly awakening people to their true potential. She inspires and encourages others to 'Development and Self Mastery,' through her own dedication to walking her own path, to the mystic beat of her own drum.

www.ingramcontent.com/pod-product-compliance
Lightning Source LLC
Chambersburg PA
CBHW031417290426
44110CB00011B/423